DUE

Obligato

Obligato

Untold Tales from a Life with Music

by Ira Hirschmann

Fromm International
Publishing Corporation
New York

Published in 1994 by
Fromm International Publishing Corporation,
560 Lexington Avenue, New York, NY 10022

Manufactured in the United States of America

Designed by David B. Kelley

Printed on acid-free paper

First U.S. Edition 1994

Library of Congress Cataloging–in–Publication Data
Hirschmann, Ira, 1901-1989.
Obligato: Untold tales from a life
with music / by Ira Hirschmann.
p. cm.
ISBN 0-88064-154-1 : $25.00

1. Hirschmann, Ira, 1901-1989.
ML429.H57A3 1994
780' .92 — dc20

[B]   93-49051 CIP MN

Contents

Contents

How This Book Came To Be

At a dinner party while revealing the secret machinations that had led the Board of the New York Philharmonic to reckless "dismissal" of the pre-eminent Maestro, Arturo Toscanini, I was interrupted by the guests: "Enough!" they protested, "that's just too interesting and important to lose. You must put those stories on paper and publish them before it's too late."

It was but one of many tales, bizarre, poignant and humorous, connected with music and musicians that had stirred the dinner guests to insist that my personal involvement with these key music events in our recent music history did not belong to me or any small group of people alone, but to the history of our times.

I suddenly became aware that the episodes I was so casually reciting had a meaning beyond personal "adventures" and that I might even have a moral obligation to share and perpetuate the experiences which had revolutionized my own life and had a similar effect on others. More importantly, by the very nature of its irresistible power, music had burst far beyond my personal enjoyment and spilled over with astonishingly practical results, onto my multifaceted activities in business, education and diplomatic affairs. Somehow, at decisive turns in my life, the magic of music prevailed over the false sirens of material gain. Thus the narrative becomes an American success story in reverse. Business, America's godhead, frequently becomes secondary to the musical idea. In perspective I began to see my practical endeavors as immovable objects while musical ideas flowed in endless grace. Music, I concluded, became the master of events, not the servant.

But I was still haunted by my long-held belief that music should be heard more and written about less; music is music and Mozart is better than the people who play him or write plays about him.

When I finally decided to write this book I was consoled by the awareness that the music itself would rescue me from the limitations of the written word, since music begins where words leave off; and music is more than an escape from words but is an escape into life itself. The impetus behind the creation of a living vehicle that extended the horizon of music in America had struck a chord in me which was to become decisive for my life's labor and love. It had also succeeded in lifting a hard-earned philosophy to the surface: *"Nothing is more practical than idealism."*

As the book came to life, at first I attempted to arrange the episodes in chronological order, but my efforts were thwarted by the events and characters themselves insistently weaving in and out of the episodes at different times and places.

How a great leap forward in music repertoire and standards of performance was made in America by the introduction of chamber music through the New Friends of Music and the author's signal role in it, is an important part of this book. During the tragic years of Hitler's domination over Europe, some of the world's leading artists, many of whom appear in the pages of this book, accepted our nation's ready invitation and brought the flower of their genius to our shores to open up new frontiers of music-making. Many of these artists rebuilt their careers from the hospitable stage of the New Friends of Music. Among the personalities you will meet in these pages, pictured with a close lens, in addition to Maestro Toscanini, Otto Klemperer, and Artur Schnabel, are: Bruno Walter, Rudolph Serkin, Béla Bartók, Jascha Heifetz, Lotte Lehmann, Arnold Schoenberg and Bronislaw Hubermann, among others who became my cherished friends. These Europeans brought to our music scene a deep cultural tradition whose roots go back for generations, whereas

Americans were obliged to approach chamber music as though it was a new discovery akin to climbing a mountain of high altitude for the first time. But they did, in addition, help to build America into what it is now, the cultural center of the world.

To a humanity looking for hope out of the disillusion, away from chaos and multiplying armaments, the distracting harmony of music may offer a detour. We will begin to recover from our material malaise the moment we take art, and particularly the art of music, as seriously as we do armaments, physics, chemistry and money.

But these tales are still bound by the vocabulary of words so limited in relation to the universal harmony of music. The last word should be left to the music itself, with a word of caution, that people who do not experience great music leave part of the universe behind.

On January 7, 1943, during World War II, in a Treasury Department broadcast appealing for the sale of War Bonds, I introduced a promising young violinist by the name of Isaac Stern, and said: "When the shrill tormented voice of Adolf Hitler has long been forgotten, we will still be drawing a full supply of happiness from the music of Wolfgang Amadeus Mozart."

Today, forty years later, Mozart's indestructible voice is heard helping to offset the crescendo of noise and disaster that threatens our very existence. Against this roar and peril, may one small voice speak up for music's timeless message of harmony? As one to whom the miracle of music has brought tranquillity, sustenance and love, it is here proffered in revelations, large and small, in the hope that the reader too will hear the secret.

Chapter One

The Secret behind the First Broadcast of the Philharmonic

Rachem

My love of music began from my earliest childhood days in Baltimore and has run as an abiding passion throughout my life. It began in my home where my sister Florence, a graduate of the Peabody Institute, gave me my first piano lesson at the age of nine. What I lacked in pianistic talent was compensated for by my enthusiasm which literally "took off" when the Baltimore Symphony Orchestra introduced "rehearsal concerts" at my high school and I heard a program which I still remember, the Wagner Overture to Tannhäuser and the Beethoven Fifth Symphony. I had my first experience with chamber music when I heard the Flonzaley Quartet at the Peabody Institute. It made an impact on me that was to have repercussions in the years to come.

When I was ten I prevailed upon my father to take me to a concert by the visiting Boston Symphony Orchestra. I can still remember hearing the Brahms Symphony No. 3 in F Major, considered an austere piece in those days, which started wheels turning in me that have never stopped. The synchronous rise and fall of the strings, the ebb and flow of the music carried me into a new world whose horizons have never ceased to expand.

My father's business as a merchant took him to New York occasionally and he would bring home programs from performances of the Metropolitan Opera. It was 1909. The magical names, which almost leapt from the pages of the programs, included Frances Alda, Enrico Caruso, Geraldine Ferrar, Tita Ruffo, Louise Homer, Antonio Scotto and Marcella Sembrich. I devoured those programs like a starving man at a feast and longed for the day when I too could hear and see those vocal luminaries in the flesh. It was my first acquaintance with the name Arturo Toscanini.

But those original first steps into the music world served only to whet my appetite for a richer musical diet. So, when a position opened up for me in Newark, New Jersey, so near to New York's cornucopia of great music, I avidly accepted it. It was there that an episode centering on music became the overture to my career in the worlds of business and public affairs.

I found myself in charge of a fund raising campaign, responsible directly to the Chairman of the Committee. He was Felix Fuld, one of the owners and the presiding officer of the famous L. Bamberger & Co. department store and the leading figure in New Jersey's business and philanthropic enterprises. He was to exert a guiding influence on my life.

In spite of the exertions my job demanded, each night I would take the hour-long trip on the Hudson Tubes to attend some music event in New York City. One evening, at the home of a friend, I heard a gifted contralto sing a moving song, "Rachem" ("Mercy" in Hebrew), which almost brought me to tears. The piece reflected the suffering of the oppressed and was sung with a rare passion. It left an unforgettable impression on me.

The fundraising campaign was to reach its climax with a gala dinner for six hundred community leaders and principle donors. The illustrious Rabbi Stephen Wise was to be the major speaker. At a planning meeting for the dinner, Mr. Fuld asked me to submit a program to ensure the success of the evening and the campaign. Here was my opportunity to do something dramatic to impress the powerful executive. I can't say how or why, but suddenly "Rachem" echoed in my ears. At that moment, a complete scenario with the song as its keynote appeared before my eyes. It called for a "collusion" between Rabbi Wise and the singer; it called for the ballroom to go dark suddenly, just as Rabbi Wise finished speaking, leaving only a single spotlight which would be centered on the face of the lovely contralto. She would begin by echoing the Rabbi's concluding word, "Rachem," on a high "G," and continue the song with its increasing poignancy to the end. Before any second thoughts could catch up with me, I phoned Rabbi Wise, explained my idea and asked him to build his appeal to a climax and end with the challenging cry "Rachem!" When he heard that the singer had accepted her role in the drama, Rabbi Wise, a showman in his own right, readily agreed.

Fuld, however, did not share my enthusiasm. He thought that the sudden darkness might cause panic in the audience. Today, I would probably agree with him, but in 1922, with youthful enthusiasm and blind confidence, I went ahead and arranged for the dramatic interlude.

At the dinner, protocol called for me to be seated with Mr. and Mrs. Fuld and the other members of the Committee. Somehow I managed to avoid Fuld's eyes when, during Rabbi Wise's address, my singer and her accompanist quietly took their places at a piano on a small balcony at the rear of the hall. Rabbi Wise's innate dramatic sense came fully into play as with all the power of his vibrant bass voice he thundered his passionate words. I could feel Fuld's eyes drilling into me as the long-maned Wise spread his arms wide, held out his open-palmed hands in supplication, and with a measured beat poured forth his peroration, "Lord, give us Mercy, Rachem!"

The electrician could not possibly have timed his move better, nor could the singer have hit the high "G" with any greater clarity or passion. As one, the audience turned to face her and, almost as if they had been subjected to mass hypnosis, froze into immobility as she sang the mournful but courageous words.

When the lights went back up, the ballroom rocked with applause as the audience exploded in a sudden release of their pent-up emotions. Most important, the money rolled in.

Only at the end of the evening, after the final tally of the funds, did Fuld speak to me. In typical clipped phrases he said:

"You had your nerve, young man; you're lucky it worked. Congratulations!"

The Founding of Radio Station WOR

My personal campaign to win Fuld's approval had succeeded. Next day, the fundraising drive over and a big success, he offered me a job in the Bamberger store and suggested that I take a position in merchandising where, he told me, the money was to be made. But I yearned for a more creative atmosphere and insisted on being placed in the advertising department. There, as the new low man on the totem pole, I was given only the leftover items of copywriting to do, for advertising the less important merchandise.

The basic material for writing the ads was submitted to us by the store's buyers, who wrote descriptions of their wares on long yellow pads. I can still see the words that were to direct my life into new and unforeseen channels scrawled in soft pencil across the face of one of those yellow sheets: "Wireless Sets with Earphones." Intrigued and uncertain about what a wireless set with earphones might be, I went down to the department that had them for sale. By working the knobs carefully and listening intently with my earphones, I was soon able to pick up the weak signal of radio station WEAF. Once I had heard the tinkling sounds of piano music which I was able to wrest from the mysterious box, my imagination was on fire. The clerk behind the counter was very helpful. His name was Jack Poppele. A former engineer, he answered all my many questions about the technical requirements for transmitting sounds through the air and about building a radio station. Poppele became an indispensable ally and later joined with me and a few others in the store in an effort to sell Fuld on the idea of applying for a license and obtaining a radio broadcasting station for the Bamberger store.

Securing a broadcast license in those days was a relatively simple matter. There was as yet no Federal Communications Commission (FCC). The sole arbiter was the Secretary of Commerce, an office held at the time by Herbert Hoover. A few forms were filled out in Washington, some questions asked and answered, and the license was issued. A location for the transmitter was found in Kearney, N.J., and with the engineering skills of Jack Poppele, it was quickly constructed. Within a few short months a new radio station was born, WOR-710 on the AM dial.

As there was no budget for program material at the station's beginning, I turned to the phonograph record department in the store and made daily lists of records of classical music to fill out the broadcast hours, interspersed with announcements of the name of the store and its slogan, "One of America's Great Stores." Commercial messages as we now know them were as yet a remote idea. Next to the phonograph department, I had a small glass partition built which served as the station's first "studio." Later, as radio sets began appearing in increasing numbers of homes, I introduced educational and entertainment programs and selling messages for the store's merchandise.

I never actually managed WOR, but my involvement in its policy-making as Advertising Manager of Bamberger's was an integral factor in its development. However, as it reached only a local audience and the sale of time for commercial advertising had not yet been introduced into the broadcast industry, the station operated at an annual loss of about $150,000. Advocates of the station's continuance were hard pressed to justify it to the store's management. Eventually, WOR expanded and developed into one of the nation's most powerful and successful radio stations.

Broadcasting Live Symphony Music

"Who wants to listen to symphony music? Ridiculous! It's for the educated few!"

I was facing Felix Fuld in his office at the Bamberger store. An imposing figure, his clipped gray mustache matched the staccato of his speech with the slight Teutonic accent he had imported from his birthplace in Frankfurt, Germany.

"By placing a WOR microphone on the stage in front of the Philharmonic," I urged, "instead of being limited to an audience of 2,700 in Carnegie Hall, the music would reach thousands in their homes who would identify the store with the prestigious orchestra and the great music."

It was 1922. Radio was still in its infancy. No one had yet dreamed of using it to bring music directly from the concert stage into thousands of homes. The idea had come to me one evening while at a Philharmonic concert in Carnegie Hall.* I had looked down from my perch in the top balcony and spotted Mr. and Mrs. Fuld sitting in a box far below.

In my enthusiasm I could hardly wait to explain my broadcast idea to Fuld and approached him first thing the next morning as he entered his office. His unqualified rejection of my idea surprised me, but I was not entirely discouraged. I politely pointed out how much it would benefit a fledgling radio station to be identified with the world's greatest symphony orchestra. But Fuld not only remained adamant, he went further to carry out his rejection. A master executive, he was no man to let a youthful employee with a harebrained scheme get away without being taught a lesson. He rang for his secretary and directed her to gather about a dozen employees from the nearby clerical staff and assemble them in his office.

In a few minutes a dozen young women were standing before him, pale with fear, all searching their memories and consciences for possible wrongdoings. Fuld wasted no time. "Young ladies," he said, "if you could hear symphony concerts on the radio, would you listen?" To his astonishment and my great relief, they all replied in unison, "Yes, sir."

---

* At that time, the price of a ticket for standing room in the upper balcony of Carnegie Hall was twenty-five cents, which I often did not have. By casing the outside of the Hall, I had discovered a secret door on the Seventh Avenue side of the building, through which I managed to squeeze unseen into the Hall. When some years later I was proposed for membership on the Philharmonic Board, in my acceptance speech I referred to my long "descent" from the upper balcony to the Board Room. But in the hope that some other youthful music lover without funds might discover the secret door and gain access to the Hall, I did not mention its location.

Sensing his embarrassment, I began to search for an inconspicuous way to remove myself from his office. Fuld dismissed the women, turned to me and said, "I still think it's a damn fool idea."

I had resigned myself to shelving my broadcast idea when the next morning the phone rang in my cubby hole office in the advertising department. It was Mrs. Fuld, the wife of the store's president.

"Last night at dinner my husband told me about your idea for broadcasting the Philharmonic concerts," she said. "How much would it cost?" I told her that I had made inquiries with Arthur Judson, manager of the Philharmonic, and that it would cost about $15,000 for the entire season.

"Is that all?" was her comment. "Go ahead and arrange for the broadcasts, but never mention my name in connection with them." She ended the conversation with the admonition, "Remember this, young man: Men have no imagination!"

As I recall, the costs were later defrayed by the company, but it was her initial support that gained approval for my plan and signaled the first broadcast by a major symphony orchestra directly from the stage in the United States and possibly in the world. It was the forerunner of countless future symphony concert broadcasts in major cities everywhere for audiences who number in the millions.

As the pioneer in the field, WOR acquired a cachet of leadership which launched it on its way to becoming one of the nation's leading and most important radio stations.

Prior to the first broadcast, we held a session to discuss what to put on the air during the approximate fifteen-minute intermission of the concert. I proposed that we use the time for an informal talk about the evening's music which could serve as vocal program notes and elected myself to write the script which the WOR announcer would read on the air.

At one of the early broadcasts, while I was chatting with friends in the lobby of Carnegie Hall, suddenly our engineer appeared, grabbed my arm and exclaimed during the intermission: "Quick, the conductor has decided to take an extra five minutes rest, the announcer has run out of material; he is stuttering and stammering, trying to think of something to say." I plowed through the crowd in the lobby and arrived in the little alcove next to the stage where I found the announcer, his brow beaded with perspiration, stumbling through some impromptu remarks. The conductor, William Mengelberg, had decided that after a fifty-two minute rendition of a Bruckner symphony he needed a longer rest than had been planned, and my written script could not be stretched. I sat down at the microphone and began by saying that I was not fond of the length of Bruckner's music and could well understand why Mr. Mengelberg needed a longer rest than we had anticipated. I asked my audience if they agreed, and invited them to write their opinions to the station. I continued in this vein until at last I saw the conductor emerge from the wings and make his way back to the podium.

The crisis was over. The next day WOR was deluged by mail from the listeners, most of it expressing appreciation of my frankness and requesting more such informal talks. I carried on my intermission talks as an extracurricular activity for a number of years until I was succeeded by Olin Downes, music critic of *The New York Times*. The talks did provide me with a medium to air many of my favorite ideas on music. During one intermission I seized the opportunity to refer to the three permanent B's— Bach, Beethoven and *Berlioz*. The next day brought a snowstorm of mail to the station with admonitions ranging from polite complaints to firm corrections of my "error" in substituting Berlioz for Brahms as the last name in the eminent trio.

The truth, of course, is that it was no error at all but deliberate, a rare opportunity to associate the name of Hector Berlioz with the two German immortals. In my efforts to bring the neglected music of the French genius to the forefront of the music public, I was grateful that his name also began with a "B." It took just this surprise shock treatment to awaken listeners to an awareness of the transcendent quality of the Berlioz scores which have since expanded the horizons of great music.

The weekly talks gave me the opportunity to share my musical thoughts with thousands of listeners. The preparation required intensive research into the background of each program's music, which was a relief from my more mundane activities in Bamberger's advertising department. It opened up a reservoir of information on composers and their works, which has served me as a valuable musical education. In addition, I was given the privilege of attending the "closed" rehearsals of the Philharmonic orchestra. To sit in the wings at performances, less than twenty feet from the podium, and to follow with my own musical score the directions of some of the world's master conductors, was a priceless experience. My favorites among the Philharmonic's conductors were: Bruno Walter, Otto Klemperer, and my special hero, Maestro Arturo Toscanini.

One Sunday afternoon, while in the midst of broadcasting my intermission talk, I inadvertently made my stage debut. An overzealous stagehand was preparing for the soloist in the second half of the program and forgot that I was seated behind a curtain in the wings. Engrossed in his effort to push a concert grand piano onto the stage, he propelled it right through my spot. The nose of the piano carried me, my table and my microphone right out onto the stage just as I was discussing the third movement of the symphony played that day. Though lying prone on the floor of the stage I had the presence of mind to hold onto the microphone into which I managed to say, "And that, ladies and gentlemen, was the strangest movement of them all."

When in February of 1929 Felix Fuld died, the soul and direction went out of the store. My personal loss was immeasurable. His partner, Louis Bamberger, a man of seventy-five who had left the management of the store entirely to Fuld, was forlorn. He was one of the few who foresaw the coming stock market crash and great depression, so when the Straus brothers, owners of R. H. Macy, made him an offer for Bamberger's, he quickly accepted it.

I learned to my amazement that the Straus brothers planned to dispose of WOR almost immediately, because as they explained to me at our very first meeting, "We do not believe in radio broadcasting." To their good fortune, I managed to persuade them to hold on to WOR for a while, and some years later they sold the station at an immense profit.

Downhearted by the sale of the store into which I had poured so much of myself, I went to see Mr. Bamberger in a state of lament. When I mentioned that my feeling about the loss of WOR was like losing "my baby," the expression in his eyes suddenly changed. "My goodness," he said on a note of dismay, "I could have sold the store and kept WOR; the Straus brothers did not want it and I could have offered it to you and your associates." He seemed genuinely regretful. However, broadcasting was in my blood. I had already begun experimenting with television and I was destined to pioneer in FM with a radio station of my own.

Chapter Two

Creation of the New Friends of Music

Opening New Frontiers of Music

I t was in 1936 that I was able to fulfill a dream which extended the frontiers of music-making in America to include the sublime literature of chamber music. I created the New Friends of Music.* In retrospect it seems incredible that until then the inexhaustible repertoire of chamber music was still a secret to the vast music-loving audiences of America.

The idea of presenting chamber music in regular cycles in annual concerts had begun to germinate in me when attendance at the Sunday chamber music evenings in my home on Gramercy Park in New York City had expanded beyond the capacity of my large living room. It was evident that there was a hunger and a need for a public vehicle to expose to growing audiences the basic literature of chamber music, heretofore considered esoteric and reserved for the musical elite with developed taste.

Later, when I heard Beethoven's twelve trios played by Artur Schnabel, Bronislaw Hubermann and Emanuel Feuermann in the intimacy of a hotel suite in New York, my imagination was on fire.

Hearing these masterpieces performed at close range by consummate artists who seemed to be sharing a secret message with each other exercised a powerful effect on me. Caught in the magnetic spell of music achieved

---

* In the early 1900s, only two established chamber music quartets existed in all America. They were the Flonzalay and the Kneisal Quartets.

by only three instruments, I asked myself, "Should this heavenly music in such a concentrated form be denied to the myriad of music lovers who would embrace it and whose lives it would enrich? What other sublime music composed for small combinations of instruments must be waiting, almost beckoning, to be brought to life?"

I decided to research the complete literature of chamber music works by the great composers. Out of it came the startling revelation that a predominant share and variety of classical music did not belong to the larger forms, symphonies, choruses and opera, but had been composed for small combinations of instruments, for solo and limited ensembles and principally for string players. It was clear that the plethora of riches awaited us. The New Friends of Music became the logical solution.

It might have seemed sensible to experiment with one or two concerts first, to test the interest and availability of regular audiences for chamber music. But I persisted in the belief that among the more than seven million people in the New York Metropolitan area there must exist at least 1,500 souls (the capacity of Town Hall) who would prefer to be on the side of the angels with the best of chamber music being performed by the finest artists and presented at a price they could afford to pay. The establishment of another permanent body for the vast literature of chamber music in addition to the New York Philharmonic and the Metropolitan Opera would fill a void.

Since chamber music is lean and spare in form, it followed that it should be presented in a similar manner, without a Board or a Committee—in effect as a one-man operation which would guarantee that no elements foreign to the nature of the music could creep in; that this pure, compact, elevated music would have the freedom it demanded to play out its role unhampered by any outside trappings.

My concept was to present full cycles covering the major works of one to three composers each season, in a series of from sixteen to twenty concerts a year, until the entire major literature of chamber music had been covered.

Before embarking on the venture I decided to test my idea and invited a group of leading musicians and music managers to my home to get their reactions. I opened the evening with the Gordon String Quartet to create a mood and provide a sample of what I was about to propose. I then outlined my plan for the New Friends of Music and asked for opinions. Everyone tried to discourage me. Some were even less than polite and branded the venture far-fetched and unrealistic. The only word of approval came not from a musician but from an old friend and music lover, Elmer Rice. Finally, I took a vote. It was twenty to one against. Announcing, "Now I'm sure that I'm right, I'm going ahead," I plunged in.

It meant breaking new ground in the concert world, a sizable investment, and a violation of the established concert format. But I ignored precedents and went ahead with an innovative formula. My task was to break down an unconscious prejudice which, over the years, had somehow fastened itself onto the term "chamber music," partly because it was offered most frequently by amateur music "buffs" in their own homes in overlong sessions which gave a distorted impression of chamber music's heavenly discourse.

In conceiving the format for the New Friends of Music, I remembered those dry, overlong sessions which had served to stigmatize the term "chamber music." It was a compelling challenge to break through those "hothouse" performances with the freshness of chamber music designed for the many instead of the few. But the glory of the music was on my side. For me it was only a matter of wedding the most palatable form of music with an equally intimate approach to it by the listeners. I was determined to bring the two together. In addition I resolved to destroy the false assumption that American music lovers lacked the sensitivity to appreciate the purity and simplicity inherent in chamber music; that only opera and symphony were within their grasp.

I made certain that the New Friends concerts were never longer than an hour and a quarter. Their programs were carefully designed with the aim of never tiring the listeners, even to the point of juxtaposing compositions in different keys to refreshen the ear. Rarely were major "heavy" works placed one after another. A refreshing variety was provided by the inclusion of lieder* (which is chamber music) on our programs, for they had too long suffered an inexplicable neglect in the nation's music repertoire. They were usually placed midpoint in the programs between numbers for strings or in concerts of full lieder cycles.

From the beginning I put the emphasis where it belonged, on the composer first and the performer second. To me, the performer occupies a fortunate and transitory place in recreating the composer's message, which will live on long after the momentary performance. To repeat Artur Schnabel's apt aphorism, "Beethoven is better than the people who play him."

I went to great lengths to be faithful to this philosophy, by placing the names of the composers first and in large letters on all our programs and announcements, with the names of the performers below in smaller, readable type.

I even wrote a script which I gave to the secretary in the New Friends office with instructions to read it word for word when replying to telephone inquiries regarding the name of the performer in the coming week's concert. A typical replay would read:

Caller:	Who will be playing at next Sunday's concert?
Secretary:	Beethoven.
Caller:	No, I mean who will be playing?

---

* The German word "lied" (art song) derives from German poems intended for singing which reflect the love of nature found in the lyrics of Goethe, Schiller, Heine and Möricke. The forerunners of the composers of lieder were Bach, Haydn, Mozart, Beethoven and Weber. Other composers who immortalized the lied were Schumann, Mendelssohn, Brahms, Hugo Wolf and Richard Strauss, but the greatest exponent was Franz Schubert, who translated 800 poems (120 in one year) into incomparable lyrical music for combined piano and voice.

Few music lovers are aware that lieder constitute an integral, indispensible part of chamber music. Some of classical music's most indestructible jewels belong to this genre. An occasional recital by a "star" performer would include a few of Franz Schubert's gems, but the glory of the lieder's magical life in music had for too long been kept distant from American music lovers. The fusion of the dramatic lyrical song is enhanced by the partnership of the piano into a feeling of oneness, from exalted revelations to carefully guarded secrets. When performed by vocalists and pianists worthy of the poetical subject, the results can be the most poignant experience possible in music.

Secretary: Artur Schnabel will be the fortunate intermediary
between Beethoven and the public.

After some hesitation on the other end of the line, usually the receiver would be gently hung up, but the intent of the message could not have been lost on the caller.

I wrote and published a "Statement of Aims" which promised to present complete cycles of the major works of several composers each season, including the best literature of chamber music and lieder with no "little pieces."

The complete sixteen programs and the artists were listed in advance each season. I spelled out a series of rules for both the artists and the audiences for what I termed "music-making" instead of "concert-going." All elements foreign to the music were eliminated, such as encores, applause between movements, flowers, and even intermissions, which were not necessary, as the programs were varied in character and rarely more than an hour and a quarter in length. There was to be no exploitation of artists' personalities. Free passes were outlawed to ensure that the audience would consist only of music lovers who cared enough about the music to be willing to pay to hear it.

An unusual and leisurely concert hour was chosen, 5:30 on Sunday afternoons. So that the concerts would be accessible to as many music lovers as possible, I priced all tickets at about one dollar each on a subscription basis. A number of tickets were set aside for music students at twenty-five cents per concert. No tickets to single concerts were sold to avoid attendance only at concerts with "name" artists. I believed that good music could stand on its own, and that it did not need patrons or a Board; that concerts freed from the shackles of a committee could, under careful management, be self-supporting, or operate at only a small deficit even with such low ticket prices.

I made a special point of engaging young, gifted but unknown artists, many of them Americans. They were presented in the same way as were the celebrated artists, as no special fanfare was permitted for any.

The timing of the New Friends of Music coincided with the rise of Fascism in Europe. Many of the world's leading musicians who escaped from Germany, Italy and Austria found a haven on the hospitable stage of the New Friends of Music from which they were able to renew their interrupted careers. Among them were: Artur Schnabel, Adolf Busch, Rudolph Serkin, Lotte Lehmann and Otto Klemperer, as well as such groups as the Budapest String Quartet and the Kolisch, Hungarian, and Pro Arte Quartets.

We searched the United States and throughout the world to find musicians whose artistry was particularly suited to each piece. I had heard of a promising pianist in Vienna and located him in Basel-Riehen, Switzerland, at the home of his father-in-law, Adolf Busch, the celebrated violinist. His name was Rudolph Serkin, and I invited him along with the Busch Quartet to come to America and appear before the chamber music audiences of the New Friends of Music.

The programs were developed after months of study and planning with my wife and collaborator, Hortense Monath, to provide unity and balance, and to sustain the audience's interest. They were announced in advance each season with the names of the performers. The works to be played were assigned to the artists who in all cases accepted them. In addition to the better known works of chamber music, many that had rarely been performed were given, such as Mozart's sextets for strings and two horns, his sonata for cello and bassoon; Schubert's Octet, his Arpeggione sonata and his two great cycles, "Die schöne Mullerin," and "Die Winterreise," as well as Schumann's "Dichterliebe" and "Frauenliebe und Leben." We also introduced works by contemporary composers. The initial performances of all of Béla Bartók's string quartets were played by the then neophyte Juilliard String Quartet in a series of four New Friends of Music concerts.

I engaged the most erudite musicologists to write our program notes, and a permanent contribution to the literature of orchestral and chamber music was made by the publication of the collected program notes in three illuminating volumes each season. Written by such musical authorities as

Herbert Peyser, Irving Kolodin, Virgil Thomson, Caesar Searchinger, Mark Brunswick, and Hans T. David, they were made available for sale to the public by the Columbia University Press. The program notes were mailed out to our subscribers in advance of each concert. As chamber music demands from the audience complete concentration on the music, this eliminated the distraction of the rustling of pages during a performance, which I abhorred. No free tickets were given to the press. While I welcomed their critical appraisal, I did not seek it. Nevertheless the critics came and enjoyed the music.

On November 8, 1936 the first concert opened with Beethoven's C-sharp Major Quartet, possibly the loftiest piece in the entire literature of chamber music. This was *unprecedented,* but our premise was that the most abstract music should be played at the beginning of the program when the audience was fresh and most receptive.

I still thrill when I recall arriving at Town Hall for the opening concert and observing the long line outside, all eager to hear chamber music. Observing their anticipation as they entered the hall was only a preliminary to my satisfaction on seeing and feeling the happiness radiating from their faces when, at the concert's end, they filed out of the aisles onto the street.

Contrary to the dire predictions of music wiseacres, ninety-six percent of the 1,500 seats in Town Hall were subscribed to in advance for the entire first season. At the end of the first season, I published a full statement of our income and cost as proof of my conviction that good music presented for its own sake could approximately pay its own way without patrons. That year, in spite of having paid their normal concert fees to such artists as Schnabel, Lotte Lehmann, and Pro Arte Quartet, Elisabeth Schumann and others of similar eminence, I lost only $408. Our deficits did mount in later years after the addition of the orchestra and with increased costs and union wages, but not appreciably. I personally directed the entire operation, for which I received no compensation. None of the supernumeraries or outside trappings which have weighed down other major music organizations were carried.

It is an interesting sidelight that when my minimal loss for the series in the first season was published, Marshall Field, then President of the New York Philharmonic Society, approached me and asked me to take over the financial management of the Philharmonic, to apply my formula toward reducing its large deficit. I replied I could not do so unless I was given complete authority over all aspects of management. It would have meant running head-on into Arthur Judson and the social amenities of the Board, which I abjured.

A retrospective look at the printed programs of the New Friends of Music concerts is refreshing and instructive. The programs, along with other related data on the New Friends of Music, have been presented to the Music Library at Lincoln Center, where they have a permanent residence and are available to the public for review. The few sample programs shown here, selected at random, cannot fail to arouse a feeling of nostalgia and a yearning for concerts today with programs of a similar caliber.

In addition to the members of our audiences, music critics spoke with appreciation of the treasures of music which were being exhumed and made accessible to a public which was hungry for them.

"I cannot understand why this audience should be different from audiences at other concerts, yet it undoubtedly is," wrote Samuel Chotzinoff in *The New York Post*. "It is silent, eager, and thoroughly absorbed in what is going on. Yesterday I felt a curious excitement at being part of that packed house where all listened to the music of Brahms as if it was a revelation."

In the second season of the New Friends, a joint project with the RCA corporation was inaugurated for recording a major portion of the New Friends concerts simultaneously with their performance at Town Hall. For the first time, music which formerly could be heard and enjoyed only by the 1,500 people who could be accommodated by Town Hall was now available on records and could be heard by thousands in their homes exactly as it had been performed for the New York audience.

Until the third season, the concerts were accessible only to listeners living within the Greater New York area. At that time the broadcasts of the concerts were begun, first over radio station WQXR and later over my own FM station, WABF. In the 1940s our listening audience was broadened to extend to music lovers in cities throughout the country. With the collaboration of David Sarnoff it was arranged for a full hour of each concert to be presented over NBC's coast-to-coast network on Sunday afternoons. During the war years NBC broadcast the concerts via short wave to our soldiers overseas. Thus the chamber music concerts of the New Friends of Music, along with the NBC Symphony Orchestra and the Metropolitan Opera became this nation's major music broadcast institutions.

Gradually, the format of the New Friends of Music concerts was copied in other cities across the nation, some with my assistance, and chamber music began to be heard in concert halls throughout the country. The broad acceptance of the concerts over a period of eighteen years exploded, once and for all, the myth that American music lovers lacked the background and seriousness for this purest form of music, particularly considering the joy and alacrity with which they embraced it when it was made available to them in a palatable form by the New Friends of Music.

Listening to the last five string quartets of Beethoven is an experience of power and pathos nearly unendurable. To be exposed to those distilled utterances recreated by four string instruments is to be involved in the most poignant, transcendent communication, to enter another world, an undiscovered country. What cruel verdict kept the composer's very heart from bursting as he rose to those ethereal heights and knew that his total deafness would deny him the right and joy of hearing those heavenly sounds? And to think that these are but five of the sublime pieces awaiting, if not beckoning, from an almost endless treasure of music in this genre.

The Orchestra of the New Friends of Music

In our fourth season we decided to expand the repertoire of our concerts to include the neglected store of chamber music masterpieces composed for small orchestra. As no ready ensemble of the size existed for this music it became necessary for us to create a small orchestra of our own. Now this vast literature, an inseparable part of chamber music, would be accessible to the public performed by an ensemble of the size designated by the composer.

The New Friends of Music Orchestra, while musically a fully dimensioned symphony with a personnel of from thirty-two to forty, was a chamber ensemble and did not compete with the regular mammoth symphony orchestras with more than one hundred players. It was the first musical body of its size in America, although similar groups had for centuries been an indispensable part of European musical life.[*]

The large standard orchestras omitted from their programs many of the great works of Bach, Haydn and Mozart, which were composed for small orchestra. When they did occasionally perform some of these pieces they would reduce the number of players in an effort to achieve the pure sound of a small ensemble. The result was a big sound compressed instead of the fusion of sound from the rehearsed interplay of instruments created by a chamber music ensemble.

The Orchestra's first programs were to comprise the six Brandenberg concerti of Bach performed in two successive concerts and conducted by Otto Klemperer, one of the world's eminent conductors and a special favorite of mine. I had engaged Klemperer to build the orchestra from among the best and most talented young American players available. Such an orchestra, under the direction of one of the masters of the European school of conduction, gave promise of becoming a unique ensemble with fresh vitality and spirit. But before Klemperer could begin to form the orchestra, he suffered a stroke (from which he later recovered). To replace him, Artur Schnabel suggested Fritz

---

[*] When Beethoven conducted his own symphonies in the early 1800s his full orchestra consisted of forty-six players.

Stiedry, former conductor of the Städtische Oper in Berlin, where he had succeeded Bruno Walter. I accepted Stiedry, whose musical qualifications proved to be of the highest order. He selected the players for the orchestra after a long and arduous series of auditions. Eighty-five percent of those chosen were American-born, with an average age of twenty-five. Five young women were included on the roster, for the first time three of them as first desk players — the first horn, the first oboe, and the first flute. Both Frances Blaisdell, first flutist, and Lois Wann, first oboist, developed later into top-ranking artists as solo performers throughout the country.

Stiedry succeeded in building a spirited ensemble. In spite of a floundering beat, his sensitive musical taste communicated itself infectiously to the young players, creating a vibrant, pulsating sonority ideally suited to the concentrated orchestral scores of Bach, Haydn, Mozart, and the early Schubert.

Unfortunately, Stiedry's great gifts as a musician were compromised by his unstable personality. I was frequently plagued by unwarranted crises he created with temperamental outbursts. His worst infraction came when I invited Mayor La Guardia to be the intermission speaker at the orchestra's first "rehearsal-concert" at the new High School of Music and Art, in a program to be performed at Town Hall the following evening. At the very last moment, for some unknown reason, Stiedry refused to conduct; only the fact of the Mayor's attendance brought him back to the podium. But the Mayor, who had a low tolerance for the temperamental antics of others, refused to speak to him, then or later.

In spite of his temperament, however, Stiedry managed to infuse the young orchestra with a pure and palpitating spirit that captivated audiences and won highest praises from the critics. With its first appearance, in a program of three of Bach's Brandenberg concerti, the orchestra established itself as a young, vibrant, and authoritative musical body. The enthusiastic response was reflected in the comments of New York's leading music critics.

In *The New York Herald Tribune* of December 16, 1940, Virgil Thomson*
wrote:

> It was a happy day for us all when the New Friends of Music took to giving
> orchestral concerts. This society is not bound to formulae either of
> repertory or of sonority as the great foundations are. It is not enchained
> to the monumental symphony or enslaved to the heroic style. It does-
> n't have to please anybody but musicians and it doesn't have to impress
> anybody at all. Naturally, once that bondage is broken, there is an infin-
> ity of beautiful music to play. *Long may the New Friends continue their
> superb performance of great music old and new!*

In *The New York Times,* music critic Olin Downes wrote:

> The spirit of the playing fell upon the ears with a refreshing lustiness,
> and with a swing and glow of tone like a fresh wind from the forest or sea.
> No such simple orchestral playing has been heard for a long time, and
> none ever more truly inhabited by the spirit of youth.

In *The New York Sun,* veteran music critic Oscar Thompson devoted his
weekly column to the opening performance of the Orchestra and was lyrical in his praise:

> Bach-playing of an infectious enthusiasm delighted an audience of capac-
> ity proportions in Town Hall. It served to introduce, under auspicious
> circumstances, the Orchestra of the New Friends of Music and its con-
> ductor, Fritz Stiedry. . . .
>
> The ensemble has the look of youth and the playing tended to con-
> firm appearances. It was lusty and forthright, with a healthy muscular-
> ity of attack and tone particularly appropriate to the music played. . . .

---

* When Lawrence Gilman, the poetic and profound music critic of *The New York Herald
Tribune,* died, Geoffrey Parsons, the editor, and Helen Rogers Reid, the great lady who was
the publisher of *The Herald Tribune*, selected Virgil Thomson, a gifted, young, Parisian-
born composer and writer, to succeed him.

Thomson's reviews rocked the music world and created a mild sensation. The stuffiness
and rigid adherence to the status quo which had for too long dominated the musical scene
reeled from the thrusts of his well-aimed lance, in all instances deserved and overdue.

For me, Thomson was a fresh breeze on the foggy music scene, and he could not have
come at a more timely hour. Artists were among the first victims of the political ferment
in Europe just prior to World War II, and their flight to America was in full swing.

Thomson, with his sensitive ear, pen, and unimpeachable integrity, had arrived on the
scene at a fortuitous hour for the New Friends of Music. While not all of his reviews of
our concerts were laudatory, he did understand the keynote of our music endeavors, and
sensed our reach for music's inner voice, our avoidance of all aspects of virtuoso display
and our hope to involve our audiences in the music's intentions.

In later years the Orchestra went on tours of many of the Midwest cities where the pure program fare was a novelty to the music lovers who until then had been fed only standard, oft-repeated, "sure-fire" programming.

Beginning with its third season, the concerts of the New Friends Orchestra were broadcast live over the NBC radio network. These broadcasts enabled the Orchestra to provide a vast public with a new repertoire of symphonic chamber music, which was presented without interruption for commercial announcement. The enthusiastic response from all parts of the country more than confirmed my contention that American music lovers had been long shortchanged by the concert managers, who, having a low opinion of their tastes, fed them a low-grade, parochial music diet.

Everywhere the Orchestra performed, audiences responded wholeheartedly to the new experience of hearing classical chamber music played by an ensemble of the size for which it had been composed. Newspaper reviews in city after city testified to the happy reaction of audiences to the new horizons of music the programs opened up for them.

"No longer must we relegate eighteenth-century music to musicologists and history books," wrote one critic in Oberlin, Ohio, where the orchestra had presented three concerts in two days. "A century of music, long tucked away, has now found in the orchestra of the New Friends of Music, an ally, one capable of restoring it to life, as fresh and stimulating as on the day it was conceived."

"The spirit was that of a music festival," said another commentator.

I assumed the full financial burden of the orchestra alone, perhaps naively. That this was somewhat unbelievable was brought home to me by David Sarnoff, President of RCA.

One evening at Town Hall, he attended a concert of the orchestra as my guest. During the intermission he took the opportunity to go backstage to observe his announcers broadcasting nationally and to the soldiers overseas. When in answer to his casual question as to what group or institution supported the orchestra, I replied, "I do it, myself," he nearly gasped. "Impossible!" he declared incredulously. Looking back on Sarnoff's reaction I realize that it was born of bewilderment, for he knew I was a salaried executive without a reservoir of corporate funds behind me.

In 1940 the New Friends Orchestra made history by presenting the world premiere of a two-movement *Kammersymphonie* by the renowned composer Arnold Schoenberg, the inventor of the twelve-tone scale and one of the great creative geniuses of the twentieth century. After I had requested that Stiedry try to locate an original composition, he told me that his friend Schoenberg had written the first movement of a *kammer* (chamber) symphony in 1906. He had left it unfinished and had told Stiedry that he was prepared to write the second and final movement, but that a sponsor was required. I immediately expressed interest in financing the completion of the symphony. My recollection is that the price was a thousand dollars with the stipulation that the New Friends Orchestra would give the symphony its world premiere.

Schoenberg volunteered to dedicate the piece to me (I have never seen nor sought out the exact dedication). The work was completed in 1940 as Kammersymphonie No. 2, Opus 38. In it the technique of the twelve-tone method and the variants contained in the different mirror forms of the thematic material are radically employed, so that the second movement particularly is technically representative of the later Schoenberg.

Schoenberg arrived in New York a few days before the performance, and I met with him at the Hotel Algonquin on West Forty-fourth Street. Short in stature with an impressive personality, his penetrating eyes seemed to drill into me as he gave staccato answers to my deferential questions.

Why, I asked, had he confined the piece to two movements? Only Schubert had done this with his "Unfinished Symphony," and the mystery of why has never been solved.

Schoenberg's reply over the tea cups was graphic and unambiguous. "You see this?" he asked, holding up his left hand. "It has five fingers and is complete as it is. Would you want me to add another finger or two?" There was no doubt that my question, never designed to intrude into the composer's anatomy or private world of creation, had been answered with finality. The symphony was accorded a brilliant performance by Stiedry and his fledgling orchestra and is now a part of the standard repertoire of chamber music.

Schoenberg later made one unscheduled appearance with the New Friends Orchestra as conductor of one of his works, "Verklärte Nacht." It came about as the result of one of Stiedry's tantrums. A few days before the scheduled performance of this difficult piece, a message was slipped to me during an executive meeting at Bloomingdale's, where I was vice president at the time. The message stated that Stiedry had just walked out in the middle of a rehearsal. I scribbled a note and gave it to the waiting secretary. "Phone Schoenberg in California and engage him for Sunday."

His fee and travel expenses, as I recall, were not excessive, and flying him to New York rescued me from a tenuous situation, as no other conductor could have interpreted the complex work at such short notice.

A few days later Schoenberg wrote me a letter so appreciative and heartwarming that I am sharing its full contents with my readers (see illustration).

It was perhaps in the relationship between the players and the listeners that the concerts of the New Friends of Music differed most from average symphony concerts. The appreciation and enthusiasm of our audiences could not be better expressed than in the words of a letter we received towards the end of the 1941 season:

> ... meanwhile I take this occasion to thank you for your services to the cause of the greatest music, and to wish you every success in the seasons to come. You have spread the gospel of chamber music over our whole country in an incredibly short time. Only great music could win its way so quickly and so enduringly. ...

Chamber music in the public concert halls today is generally acknowledged to have been initiated by the New Friends of Music, which succeeded in lifting it out of the drawing rooms of the few for the many. For me the concerts were decidedly a labor of love. I could personally plan and hear all the great music for which I yearned, and have the additional joy of sharing it with my "friends of music." The success of the concerts also nailed down the truth of my conviction that people will listen to all music but will prefer the best.

There was a social implication to the avid acceptance of chamber music by adherents of the New Friends of Music that cannot be overlooked. It proved once and for all that American music lovers were not only prepared, but in fact were acutely hungry for the pure fare of chamber music. When the acceptance of chamber music came, after the New Friends had broken the ground, it came in an avalanche. Today, chamber music has become an inseparable part of our musical life.[*] It is, however, my belief that this could not have come about in so short a time had the New Friends not opened a door and offered a hospitable platform on which it introduced full cycles of the best of chamber music. Without my New Friends of Music concerts, music-making might have lost a golden moment in history, tantamount to a squandered opportunity in time.

Today, as this is being written, more than thirty years after the New Friends of Music concerts, I still frequently encounter "friends of music" who cherish the memory of those concerts, who are effusive in their expressions of gratitude for all they had meant to them, and who urge me to resume them.

It is always satisfying to hear that the concerts are so warmly remembered, and to know that I was instrumental in bringing the repertoire of chamber music's sublime literature to the general public and thus sharing it with so many old and new friends of music.

---

[*] The Chamber Music Society of New York is a direct outgrowth of the audiences established by the New Friends of Music.

How the Budapest String Quartet Came to America

In the second season of the New Friends of Music, after hearing several of their recordings, I engaged a new string quartet that had been winning wide acclaim in Europe. Their playing seemed so exceptional that I violated my rule against including any artists whom I had not previously heard perform. It was the Budapest String Quartet.

The day before their first concert was scheduled, I received a phone call from a U.S. Immigration Department official at Ellis Island. He informed me that the four musicians had arrived but were being detained, as their papers were not in order. It was Saturday morning; their concert was to take place the following evening; I had to get them off Ellis Island immediately. In desperation, I phoned my friend Mayor La Guardia at his home.

"Coming to the concert tomorrow evening?" I asked him.

"Yes," he said, "why?"

"You *think* you are," I replied and went on to explain about the quartet being detained on Ellis Island, suggesting that his friend Ed Corsi, who was in charge on Ellis Island, might help. The Mayor, a great prankster, seemed tickled by my discomfiture, he laughed and hung up. It was only after repeated efforts that I was able to get him back on the phone. When I finally reached him, he whispered in a conspiratorial voice, as though including me in some dark plot, "Ira, I have an idea. Why go to a lot of bother? You and I can take a boat out to Ellis Island, enjoy the concert there all by ourselves." I groaned as he again hung up the phone. However, he did call his friend, and Ed Corsi arranged to have the four musicians brought to Town Hall on Sunday afternoon. They were escorted by a marshal who waited backstage during the performance and immediately upon its conclusion whisked them back to Ellis Island. They were finally released later that week.

In their performance that evening, especially under the trying circumstances, the Budapest String Quartet more than lived up to its European reputation. In subsequent years, concerts by the Budapest String Quartet became centerpieces of each season's New Friends of Music concert series, and they established themselves as the leading string quartet of the day. Laurels are due to Mischa Schneider and his incomparable colleagues who set a standard of chamber music performances which today is emulated by such masterful ensembles as the Guarneri, Juilliard, Tokyo, Cleveland and Amadeus, among others.

The New Friends of Music brought every first-class European string quartet to America, including the Pro Arte, Paganini, Hungarian, Kolisch, Roth, Busch, Amadeus, and the Quartet Italiano. Among the American ensembles we introduced were the Gordon, Fine Arts, Stradivarius, Musical Art, and the Albenieri Trio.

The appearance of an ensemble under the auspices of the New Friends of Music in New York provided it with a cachet of prestige for engagements in many other cities, thereby spreading the gospel of chamber music throughout the nation.

"Winterreise" with Lotte Lehmann

Among the ground rules I had laid down for the New Friends of Music concerts was that all artists were to appear in the same way, with no special fanfare or treatment. But there were a few occasions when I was obliged to cope with objections to this rule by famous artists and their managers. My severest test came with Mme. Lotte Lehmann, an artist who brought everything she sang to life and was my favorite lieder singer. She was one of the few artists in the world capable of understanding and vocally realizing the great lieder cycles of Schubert, Schumann and Brahms.

In 1937, after her concert for the New Friends of Music, I went backstage to the artists' room and asked her if she would sing Franz Schubert's "Winterreise" for us the following season. This supreme classic, based on an epic poem by Müller, requires an entire concert and is the severest test of the artistry of any vocalist. She looked aghast and replied, "It would take me three years to learn it." "Very well," I retorted, taking out a small note-book, "You are engaged to sing it on Sunday, April 13, 1940."

True to plan, three years later the work was announced for a concert in the 1940–41 New Friends series. On the appointed date I arrived at Town Hall fifteen minutes before the concert was to begin to check on arrangements. The Hall was filled to the last seat, including standing room. I found a mild insurrection going on backstage. Mme. Lehmann's personal manager was insisting that seats be made available on the stage for the overflow, that a red carpet be put down running from Mme. Lehmann's dressing room to the center of the stage, and that flowers were to be handed to her both before the intermission and at the conclusion of the concert. All three requests were in direct violation of my rules, and I refused to make any exception. Music was music, and all outside trappings, especially ones that lifted one artist above the others, were taboo. I turned to Mme. Lehmann and pleaded with her, but she adamantly refused to go on stage unless her conditions were met. I started the concerts on the split second of 5:34 P.M., and it was already 5:25. I could hear the buzz of anticipation from the full house beyond the curtain.

"If you do not go on stage in exactly nine minutes," I said, looking at my watch, "I will go out and announce that the concert is off, and why. Would you like to come out with me to make sure I say it correctly?" She glared at me, her eyes on fire, and said, "Very well, I will agree about the red carpet and the flowers, but I insist on your permitting people to sit on the stage."

"Why?" I implored. "Because otherwise I will be lonely," she replied, but I held my ground, and she finally assented.

An adoring audience, unaware of the minor drama that had been played out backstage and the near miss of the concert, greeted her appearance on stage tumultuously. The great artist warmed to the demands of the noble score as she sang, and when she reached the climax she soared to a transcendence. After the last notes the audience thundered its applause, and I ran backstage to offer my congratulations before her admirers arrived to besiege her. "You sang like an angel," I proclaimed over the roar of the applause still echoing from the hall. "Yes, but I was lonely," she answered, still unwilling to lose the argument even under the spell of her triumph. "You were not alone, Madame Lehmann, Schubert was with you," was my quick rejoinder.

Some months later, after a concert of the Philharmonic orchestra, I met her at a party given for Maestro Toscanini, who adored her. The "Winterreise" episode forgotten, we had a warm discussion, and she invited me to her hotel suite for tea, where I found her immersed in painting handsome designs on china plates. It was apparent that she was also a gifted painter. We became friends.

Later that month I was invited to a showing and sale of her ceramics, where I discovered a plate on which she had painted a likeness of Toscanini. I bought the plate and on impulse mailed it to the Maestro with a note asking if he might inscribe it with his signature. What more delightful souvenir of my friendship with two favorite artists could be found? But time passed, and as I did not hear from him, I forgot about it.

About six months later a large box arrived at my apartment along with a letter from the Maestro's son, Walter, which was anything but pleasant. It said, in effect, that he was happy to be rid of the plate as it had been the object of some friction in the Toscanini household. I had not realized that it was impossible to inscribe on the inner circle on the back of a china plate without first removing the glaze. At the Maestro's insistence, and with some difficulty, Walter had finally found the means of having the glaze removed from the plate on which the Maestro was then able to write an inscription.

He had painted a musical staff of four bars from the Chorale of Ludwig van Beethoven's Ninth Symphony. It read:

> To Ira,
> Seid umschlungen Millionen
> (Be embraced, you millions)

This follows in the Beethoven score with:

> Diesen Kuß der ganzen Welt.
> (This kiss to the whole world.)
> (Signed) Arturo Toscanini
> 3-25-1951

I have never been a collector of souvenirs, signatures or bibelots, but this plate, while fragile, is an indestructible and unique expression of a musical bond of friendship and is one of my life's prized possessions.

Since her painting had been the inspiration for the priceless gift, I felt I should share my joy in receiving the inscribed plate with Mme. Lehmann, and I wrote to her in California where she had retired, describing the Maestro's inscription.

Her reply appears on the opposite page. On rereading the last line in her letter, "It is sad to grow old," I like to think that she derived some solace from the knowledge that her memory would continue to remain youthful and alive through the joy she had given to her myriad friends from the vibrancy of her personality and through the recordings of her timeless and incomparable artistry.

Awakening Haydn Symphonies

Incredible as it may seem, in spite of the incontestable genius of Franz Joseph Haydn, by 1941 only six or seven of the 106 symphonies he was known to have composed had found their way into the repertoires of the world's symphony orchestras.

One afternoon, while with Maestro in his study, listening to a recording of his performance of the oft-repeated Haydn Symphony No. 96 in D Major, I casually asked the Maestro why so few of the great and prolific composer's symphonies were ever performed. I asked the question particularly because the Maestro's presentations of the few familiar Haydn works were so masterful and characterized by the lucidity and firm design of the composer's music. In reply, the Maestro shrugged his shoulders and told me that to his regret only a few of Haydn's scores were available and that he was at a loss to know why.

The mystery of the missing Haydn symphonies intrigued me, and with the availability of my New Friends Orchestra, I determined to conduct a search for them. I learned that Haydn had composed most of the symphonies while employed by Prince Nicholas the Magnificent of the Esterhazy family as Kappelmeister in his sumptuous palace in Hungary, which was said to be second in splendor only to Versailles.

In the 1700s the Esterhazys were the wealthiest and most prestigious princes in the country and were passionate music lovers. Living on their estate as Kapelemeister had provided Haydn with ideal conditions for composing.

Before leaving on a trip to Vienna later in 1941, I visited the Hungarian Consul in New York and obtained a letter of introduction to the current head of the Esterhazy family, the heir of Haydn's patrons. With it I was hospitably received at the luxurious Esterhazy estate just outside of Budapest. During the course of a fabulous luncheon, I discreetly brought up the subject of the missing symphonies. I mentioned my New Friends Orchestra and my desire to offer the long lost symphonies to the public and wondered if he could supply me with any information that might lead to their location. To my astonishment he replied, "Of course, most of them are here, gathering dust in our archives."

When I asked if I could have access to about six of them for performances in the United States, he agreed with alacrity. Encouraged by his amiability, I inquired why none of them had been released before, to which he blandly replied, "No one ever asked me."

I learned that the symphonies were without a basic score for a conductor. Haydn had not required one to conduct and apparently had written out the parts for each of the players in his chamber orchestra and placed them on the individual music stands before each performance at the Esterhazys' regular Friday night soirees, which were performed without previous rehearsal.

I left for Florence with the manuscripts of six exhumed Haydn symphonies. There I engaged Alfred Einstein, a cousin of Albert Einstein and the most celebrated musicologist of the day, to make up conductor's scores from the pages for the various instruments. When completed, the conductor's scores were to be sent to Fritz Stiedry, the conductor of the New Friends Orchestra.

When I returned to the United States I announced that the New Friends Orchestra would perform six previously unheard Haydn symphonies in a series of concerts, and that I had made a discovery comparable to uncovering lost Leonardos.

When Stiedry received the completed conductor's scores from Einstein, dates were set for the concerts and rehearsals began.

But the jinx that had held the symphonies prisoner for nearly two centuries had apparently followed them and me to America. During a Board meeting at Saks Fifth Avenue, where I was vice president, a secretary slipped me a note which read, "The union has stopped the orchestra's rehearsal of the Haydn symphonies. They insist on having the scores recopied in the United States before they will permit Dr. Stiedry to proceed. What shall we do?" I scribbled on the note, "How much would it cost?" and in a few minutes the secretary returned with the figure of $600. Since the concert had already been announced for that week with wide publicity, I approved the additional expense, which had already begun to mount.

Anticipating that a large audience would be eagerly awaiting the performance of the unearthed Haydn masterpieces, I shifted the location of the concert from Town Hall to Carnegie Hall. I invited Artur Schnabel and Bruno Walter to join me in my box at the inaugural concert to be among the first to hear the historic revival of Haydn's "lost" symphonies. To my utter disappointment the hall was half empty. I had apparently vastly overestimated the interest of American musical audiences in Franz Joseph Haydn, and that for them the music could have prolonged its slumber in the Esterhazy archives even longer.

The muted interest in the initial performance of the symphonies in no way diminished the unique character of the works. Fortunately, the RCA company perceived the musical value and historic importance of the symphonies and volunteered to record them. Today these symphonies are very much alive as part of the public domain in the extended repertoire of Haydn's symphonies.

As a footnote to my belated discovery of the hidden Haydn symphonies, I quote from the Foreword I appended to the Program Notes, sent out to New Friends of Music subscribers in advance of the concerts:

> In making available to the musical audiences of the twentieth century six Haydn symphonies hitherto inaccessible for performance, the New Friends of Music, with the cooperation of Dr. Alfred Einstein, is fulfilling one of the purposes for which its small new orchestra was founded: to expose pieces unavailable, or rarely heard in other quarters, in performances by young and vibrant groups under distinguished conductors. In the specific instance of these symphonies, it has restored to the repertory immortal works which throw a new light on Haydn, the composer, and which, through unexplained circumstances, remained buried for the one hundred and thirty years since the composer's death.

Serkin to Busch Rescue

In the sixteen years of the New Friends of Music concerts it was to be expected that some accidental events would occur which would delay or cancel a performance. Few did, but one concert which came perilously close to cancellation was a performance of Beethoven violin and piano sonatas with the celebrated violinist Adolf Busch and his son-in-law, Rudolph Serkin, both of whom I had been instrumental in bringing to this country.

In the middle of a sonata, Busch suddenly stopped playing, clutched his violin, and dragged himself painfully off the stage, obviously stricken. While the stunned audience remained in their seats, I rushed backstage where I found the stalwart violinist breathing heavily, apparently the victim of a heart attack. An ambulance came and took him to a hospital, where he later recovered.

Meanwhile the audience waited apprehensively. I was determined to continue the concert if at all possible. Serkin, in a nervous sweat, was pacing the anteroom. In response to his agitated question, "What should I do?" I told him, "Rudi, you must go on, Mr. Busch would want you to." His anguished query then was, "What should I play?" Beethoven's Appassionata came quickly to my mind. His head downcast, he agreed.

I then went on stage and announced, "Mr. Busch has suffered a mild indisposition. Mr. Serkin has agreed to play Beethoven's sonata Opus 53." I heard an audible sigh of relief from the audience, which was followed by a burst of applause. Serkin marched on stage to the piano, his head down almost as though in obeisance, and poured himself into the Beethoven masterpiece. His performance was imbued with a passion and intensity that cast a spell over the audience. Karl Ulrich Schnabel, my piano teacher, a relentless critic, was in the audience, and to this day vows it was the most remarkable rendition of the Beethoven opus he has ever heard.

Adolf Busch held a special place in my affections and regard for reasons that transcended his superb music-making. He was one of the small circle of noble artists who, though of Christian birth, resisted the blandishments of Hitler and his clique. He refused to remain in Germany and bow before the Führer as did his former colleague, Wilhelm Furtwängler. His superior gifts as an artist were matched by his character, and he chose to separate himself and his career from the odious atmosphere generated by the Nazis. With every member of his family he came to this country where, along with his Quartet, they established themselves firmly in the affections of American audiences.

Rudolph Serkin's pure standard of serious programming and performing helped fill the gap left by the passing of Artur Schnabel. From our first meeting in the home of Adolf Busch in Basel, Switzerland, when I invited them to come to America and perform with the New Friends of Music, a friendship sprang up between us. I cherish the memory of his many hours of music-making both together with the Busch Quartet and in his many solo concerts for the New Friends.

While making up the programs in advance of one season, I phoned Serkin and asked him if he would play my favorite piece in the literature of piano, the posthumous B-flat sonata of Franz Schubert. He replied that he would do so gladly if he could include in the program Bach's Goldberg Variations, a colossal hour-long piece and an immense challenge in its own right. His insistence on matching one gigantic masterpiece with another on the same program—to which I of course assented—is a measure of the artist's indestructible quality and fortitude.

Out of respect for my musical taste and judgment, Serkin paid me the high compliment of asking me to make up some programs for the unique chamber music concerts at his Marlboro Music Festival. It is the informal quality and uncompromising standards of the chamber music he has brought to the Vermont hills with his creation of the Marlboro Music Festival that will be the living heritage of one of the world's most dedicated and high-minded music personalities, identified equally for his idealism and his humility.

We are all beneficiaries of Rudolph Serkin's genius and productivity, and also that which includes his son, Peter Serkin, a concert pianist in the grand tradition of his father and a living guarantee of the continuance of the Serkin legend, on the same lofty level of music-making.

Not to Szell Mozart Short

It was a friendship of long standing between two stellar musicians who had found refuge in this country from the Nazi blight that was the source of a mild collusion with me regarding a program for the New Friends of Music concerts. They were George Szell, the superb Hungarian conductor, and Emanuel Feuermann, a master cellist from Austria.

I first met Szell at Schnabel's home in Tremezzo, Lake Como, Italy, where many artists had found sanctuary after they were compelled to leave their homes in Germany and Austria because of their Jewish birth. Later, when he came to the United States, I called on Szell to substitute for Fritz Stiedry, the gifted but temperamental conductor of the New Friends Orchestra, when he elected to perform tantrums instead of music at several rehearsals. Szell became the conductor of the Cleveland Symphony Orchestra, which he built into one of America's peerless music organizations.

Feuermann became a virtual "fixture" on the programs of the New Friends of Music concerts each season. But with the limitation of music literature for the cello, and our policy of not repeating any programs, after a while we began to run out of fresh compositions for his instrument. Feuermann, whose good humor in rehearsals served as an obligato to his music, decided to overcome this shortage of repertoire for his instrument by performing a Mozart sonata for the violin which had been transposed for the cello by his friend George Szell.

Feuermann came to see me and urged me in his most eloquent prose to include this transposed work on one of our New Friends programs. But this would have been contrary to our unbroken rule never to include superimposed transpositions of scores from one instrument to another in our concerts. Accused of being "purists," we went even further and instituted a campaign for the use of the "Urtext" (the pure text of the composer's unadulterated original manuscripts) whenever possible. This was to counteract the cheap, edited versions of compositions from publishers who often simplified the scores for easier performance in their aim for larger sales.

But Feuermann was not easily put off. He persisted in his argument for performing the adapted Mozart score until he finally asked me to spell out the reason for my refusal. To this he received my cryptic reply, "Because it would Szell Mozart short." The gentle rebuff succeeded and he left me in good spirits, saying that he would see me again with another suggestion for a program, but not for a few weeks as he was going to the hospital for minor surgery.

I never saw him again. He died on the operating table, only thirty-eight years old. As a cellist, he was second only to Pablo Casals.[*] His loss, not only as a performer but also as a key personality in the music world, is still deeply felt, and his profound musicianship, contagious wit and high spirits remain an enduring memory.

Meeting Béla Bartók

In 1941 we decided to break our format of presenting the standard works of the great eighteenth- and nineteenth-century composers by presenting six string quartets by the contemporary composer Béla Bartók. The then youthful Juilliard String Quartet seemed the ideal group to bring the spirit and rhythm of today's music to these works.

The announcement that the Bartók quartets were to be included on our programs for the season was greeted by our subscribers with something less than enthusiastic interest. But the spirited articulation of the young players of the Juilliard String Quartet converted the audiences to a new appreciation of Bartók's novel and colorful message. From those brilliant performances I learned that music in today's idiom must be performed by young musicians whose horizons are not confined to traditional formats.

Having learned of our interest in Bartók's music, his agent in New York approached me with the suggestion that the New Friends of Music should introduce the composer's newest chamber composition. It turned out to be a sonata for two pianos and an assortment of percussion instruments including three timpani, a xylophone, side drum with snares, side drum without snares, a cymbal suspended, a pair of cymbals, bass-drum, triangle, and tam-tam. It looked so interesting that I decided to open our next season with this world premiere.

The difficulty in securing first-class musicians to perform with the unique combination of instruments was second only to the problem of assembling them on the Town Hall stage and placing them in the order required by the

---

* Casals was then living in France. He had repeatedly rejected my invitations for him to perform with the New Friends of Music due to his sworn determination never to set foot in this country as long as the United States continued to recognize the Fascist General Franco as the leader of Spain.

composer. To resolve this logistical problem, I needed the cooperation and advice of Bartók himself. As he and his wife were to be the pianists at the concert, I invited him to tea at my apartment. I could solicit his advice on arranging the instruments on the stage and at the same time meet a great contemporary composer whom I greatly admired.

Bartók arrived with his manager at the appointed time. He turned out to be even more ascetic-looking in person than in his photographs. White-haired, with severely aristocratic features, he sat staring into space with large luminous eyes. Politely he took his tea. But when I questioned him about the composition or his wishes about the arrangement of the instruments, he simply pointed to his manager.

When my efforts to engage him in conversation in English proved futile, I tried French and German, both of which I knew he spoke, but with equally fruitless results. He continued to sit staring straight ahead without expression, almost as though he was in a trance. His manager amiably answered all my questions, and the arrangements for the rehearsals were made in infinite detail. When we had concluded, Bartók, still silent, rose stiffly, and without changing expression, simply shook hands, bowed slightly and left.

The performance turned out to be a spectacular success. When the curtain first parted to reveal the ascetic composer at a piano on one side of the stage with his beautiful wife at another piano on the opposite end, with an assortment of percussion instruments of every variety between them, and men standing behind the instruments with raised mallets to set them in motion, the audience burst into applause. This approbation was uproariously repeated at the concert's conclusion, but there can be no doubt that this composer speaks only through his music.

Chapter Three

Toscanini Revelations

The Philharmonic Board "Dismisses" the Maestro

In 1936, Arturo Toscanini, the most eminent conductor of our times, was fired from his post as principal conductor of the New York Philharmonic Orchestra. The secret maneuvering that led to his dismissal constitutes one of the most cynical acts of chicanery in the history of this country's musical life. Adored by the public as no other man in the world of music, his podium was cut from under him by the members of the Philharmonic Board led by the orchestra's powerful manager, Arthur Judson.* The leading impresario of his day, Judson also headed his own concert bureau, to which he had most of the orchestra conductors in the country under contract at a binding twenty percent of their fees. The Maestro, a man of severe independence, required no manager and saw no reason to pay financial tribute to Judson.

---

* Starting out as a reporter for the magazine "Musical America," the enterprising Judson had become manager of the prestigious New York Philharmonic Orchestra by 1928. He later founded his own concert bureau, the Community Concerts Corporation, a far-flung national empire linked to CBS, with which he attempted to corner the market of the concert buisness in America. As a result he became involved in a law suit and was forced to plead "nolo contendere" (no contest) and pay a fine of $26,000 before the matter was settled.

Speaking of Judson's financial arrangements with his artists, the late Kathleen Ferrier, a distinguished British soprano, once protested, "I have an average of 3,000 in my audiences, which means an income of at least $3,000. Yet all they pay me is $800, out of which I must pay $105 to an accompanist, a twenty percent manager's fee, rail travel for two (which is a colossal amount here), hotels, taxis, porters, tips and income tax!" She was but one of many who felt they were being shortchanged by the concert management under Arthur Judson.

While the public was applauding Toscanini's supreme performances at Carnegie Hall, backstage a case was being orchestrated against him by the Board led by Judson, a handsome man adored by the women who dominated the Philharmonic Board. Incredible as it may seem, in spite of the Maestro's overwhelming popularity, Judson managed to trump up enough fictitious reasons to convince the Board not to renew the contract of the peerless conductor. It was mainly a petticoat jury that convicted the Maestro and incited the Philharmonic Board to its infamous verdict.

At the close of the 1936 season, the Board announced that at the age of sixty-nine, the Maestro, for reasons of "health and age," was resigning from his post as Music Director of the New York Philharmonic Orchestra, and retiring to his home in Milan, Italy. Only a few of his friends suspected the skullduggery that had knocked the greatest living conductor off his podium at Carnegie Hall. Though we were brokenhearted, we were helpless against the machinations of Judson and his control over the obsequious members of the Philharmonic Board. The Maestro retired to his home in Milan and announced that he was returning to his first love, the cello.

My nearest contact with the Maestro had come during Philharmonic concerts when I was seated in the wings of the Carnegie Hall stage, not more than twenty feet from his podium, waiting to broadcast my intermission comments. It was a tantalizing experience when he would brush past me on his way to the dressing room for intermission, his eyes blazing, his brow dripping with perspiration. He might be muttering imprecations against one or all of the players, or after an exceedingly sunny performance I might hear him repeating softly, *"Bene, bene."* Seeing him at such close range as he conducted did nothing to explain the mystery of the power he radiated. I studied his every move, my eyes shifting from the score in front of me to his baton as he whipped it through the air in his peculiar circular pattern. The infectiousness of his rhythm and the incomparable sonority he evoked were in no way impaired by his "croaking" singing voice which, though barely audible, I could hear clearly from my vantage point. Almost near enough to touch him, I could sense his remoteness and did not dare approach him. He was so withdrawn, so much a part of the music he conjured up, that he might have been on a mountaintop. It would be some time before we would meet and become close friends.

Viewing the Maestro from the audience as he conducted, one received the impression of a magnetic leader of aristocratic bearing, whose grace of motion synchronized with the beauty of the music. In no gesture did he reveal any evidence that behind his poise and self-effacement there was a secret burning fire that could explode like a thunderbolt, should a single note or inflection from any one of the hundred players fail to fulfill his directions to the letter. Only those who witnessed the Maestro in rehearsal were privy to his sudden bursts of fury. I would see him go into a fiery rage when a player repeated a single incorrect accent. It would begin with a stamping of his foot and increase with a crescendo of Italian curses into a climax when he would smash the music stand in front of him and end with cracking his baton into small pieces and throwing them with a wild gesture at a benumbed musician.

Since my broadcasts entitled me to attend the orchestra's rehearsals, in my talk during the intermission of the concert on March 23, 1930, I decided to take my listeners behind the scenes at Carnegie Hall with a description of a rehearsal of the Philharmonic under the Maestro. I am sharing with my readers the words I broadcast over WOR on that Sunday afternoon.

> Good afternoon, ladies and gentlemen. Will you come with me behind the scenes of Carnegie Hall to a rehearsal of the Philharmonic Orchestra under Toscanini?
>
> It is ten minutes after ten o'clock in the morning. I enter the hall on tiptoe, for the rehearsal has already begun. The hall is pitch-black, emphasizing the blazing light on the stage. The sounds of the music pour out into the void of the empty hall and seem to echo back, interrupted from time to time by the beseeching voice of the conductor.
>
> I settle myself quietly in the rear of the hall next to Max Smith, a friend of Toscanini, who greets me in a hushed voice. I recognize the

strains of the Strauss tone poem, "Death and Transfiguration," which goes on evenly, uninterruptedly, for the moment. On the stage, the musicians, instead of being uniformly dressed in black-and-white tuxedos as on concert nights, are wearing street clothes. The many shades of gray, brown and blue give a patchwork effect, and I think how strange it is that such blended harmonious sound should be coming from such a spotty, variegated color setting. The Maestro, as always, is conducting without a score but with the same all-consuming fire and concentration as if he were standing before a vast audience.

Now, in the midst of a surging passage for strings and woodwinds, the conductor raps his stick against his music stand for silence. He explains the inflection of a phrase to the oboe; first he sings it for him, then conducts it for him alone; now it is accompanied by the other woodwinds and finally with the entire orchestra until the phrase is played to his satisfaction.

The composition sweeps on. Another interruption. The Maestro explains the inherent meaning of a passage; impatiently he beseeches them to play it precisely as the score before their eyes indicates. He raps imperiously with his baton, beating strict time against his music stand until finally the rhythm of the passage satisfies him. Another impatient tapping is a signal for renewed silence. The orchestra ceases to a man. Now Toscanini sings a passage for the strings, his guttural voice is filled with near despair as he beseeches, "*Cantare, cantare*" (Sing, sing). The strings repeat the passage as he sings along. With pleading gestures his arms seem to lift the sounds and magically draw them with his baton from each bow. Now another imperious, excited tapping of the stick is followed by a flood of words in a voice that cries out at high tension in a mixture of English, French and Italian. When he explodes into a rage of scalding Italian it is a sign that he is at a white heat of anger. The men sit back, trembling in mute silence. Now the stick again, finally the passage goes well and the transfiguration scene of Strauss's impassioned tone poem unfolds in a suffused radiance.

A recess of five minutes is called and the men amble off the stage for a moment of relaxation and a welcome smoke. The Maestro descends into the hall to confer with Maurice Von Praag, the personnel manager. When the men return, Toscanini asks Mr. Lange, the assistant conductor, to lead them in the last pages of the Strauss poem. He paces up and down the aisles, walking through the rows of empty seats from one side of the hall to the other, his arms moving back and forth with the music, his expression changing from benign serenity to displeasure when certain passages displease him.

I watch this man of genius with eagle eyes. His dress is impeccable, dark trousers and a black alpaca coat; with his clerical collar, striped dark trousers and soft shoes, he conveys the picture of a single silhouetted figure. From under his massive forehead piercing eyes peer out which sometimes seem to penetrate right through one and at other times seem to be looking out on endless distances. His graceful and aristocratic stance denotes total poise.

Impatiently he walks back down the aisle and returns rapidly to the podium. The music begins again with the brisk tapping of his stick, which he handles as though it were an inseparable part of his body.

In spite of my frequent proximity to the Maestro at rehearsals, I suppressed my mounting desire to meet him, resolving to do so only when an opportunity arose when I could be properly introduced to him by a mutual friend. It came about through Alfred Wallenstein, the former first cellist of the Philharmonic, whose ambition to be a conductor I fostered by engaging him to lead the Bamberger Little Symphony broadcasts over WOR.

Wallenstein invited me to a dinner to meet the Maestro and suggested that I bring a friend. The friend was Fiorello La Guardia, Mayor of New York. The two illustrious figures who reflected so much glory on their Italian heritage immediately found common ground for a spontaneous and exciting interchange.

At last I could express to the Maestro in person my ardent appreciation of his incredible music-making. At subsequent meetings it did not take long for a genuine rapport to be established between us, and I was soon included in his small coterie of intimate friends. Often after Philharmonic concerts we would gather for midnight suppers at the home of Fred and Elsa Muschenheim, a narrow brownstone connected to the Hotel Astor which they owned and in which the Maestro had an apartment on the top floor.

When the Maestro arrived at these suppers, a butler at the door would be holding a glass of champagne ready for him. For many of the guests these evenings were the most exciting gatherings in the world. In addition to the

Maestro one might find oneself seated next to Jascha Heifetz, Vladimir Horowitz, Fritz Kreisler or Lotte Lehmann, who was one of the Maestro's favorites, or some other world-famous artist. The Maestro would be seated at the head of the table with a pretty woman on each side. His eyes would flash as he talked rapidly and intensely in his hoarse, guttural voice, often mixing English with Italian.

The high point of one of his most passionate discourses, as I remember, was when he talked about his idol, Giuseppe Verdi.

"Great was Verdi!" he exclaimed, his face brightening. "He was born a *contidino,* a peasant, and remained a peasant, like me."

In 1887, the Maestro, though already a conductor, had arranged to play the cello in the orchestra at La Scala in Milan at the premiere performance of *Otello* conducted by Verdi himself.

Having had the pleasure of introducing the Maestro to my friend, Mayor La Guardia, it was gratifying for me to see the mutual regard and affection they immediately developed for one another.

La Guardia's well-known predilection for following fires marked an incident which took place during a dinner party at my home which was attended by both celebrated figures. In the middle of dinner, La Guardia was summoned by telephone to a fire. He excused himself and dashed off. I could sense the envy in Toscanini, who was aching to go with the mayor but could not bring himself to ask to be taken along. If the mayor was acting the part of the leader of a brigade without whom no fire could be quenched, the Maestro had reverted to the small boy with an irrepressible longing to chase a fire engine.

In all my years of close association with Toscanini, I never knew him to accord any artist the kind of adulation he bestowed upon La Guardia on his return from the fire.

Never at a loss to seize an opportunity for the theatrical, when the Mayor returned, he stopped short at the front of the dinner table, went through the motions of brushing off his hands, as if he had personally put out the fire, and then sat down and resumed his meal.

The relationship between the two Italians grew in warmth, and I played host to them at a number of unforgettable dinner parties.

To prepare a meal to suit both these prima donnas would challenge the skill of a White House chef. Toscanini was held in check by Margherita De Veccio, his trusted friend and protector. She insisted that no matter what the others might eat, the Maestro must have a thick soup, Italian bread sticks, and blandly cooked chicken. La Guardia, on the other hand, was a gourmet for whom nothing was too exotic.

In advance of one dinner, La Guardia mentioned that he would enjoy goulash, Viennese style, a dish for which my wife Hortense's Aunt Kathe, a fabulous cook, was justly famous.

Pleased by the opportunity to give a "command performance," she arrived from Newark two days in advance of the dinner, armed with her own utensils. The actual preparation of the goulash began twenty-four hours before dinner.

The goulash was brought to the table in a giant cauldron. The lid off, the air in the room was immediately redolent with the aroma of the herbs Aunt Kathe had so skillfully blended into her magic potion.

Toscanini sat impassively, but when finally his pallid serving of chicken was placed before him, he could not restrain himself. Shoving his plate aside, he demanded, received and ate a large portion of the goulash to the delight of Fiorello, who cheered him on to a second helping.

The two men shared a passion for red wine with their meals, and a fine cognac to top them off. In preparation for our dinners I would search the stores of New York's finest wine dealers to find a vintage bottle of cognac which they would sip until long after the dinner. After two or three snifters, the Maestro would recall and resume a battle he had fought long ago with his erstwhile friend, Gatti-Casazza, General Manager of the Metropolitan Opera Company, who had originally brought him to the United States. Toscanini had enjoyed his years at the Met, where his baton had conducted Caruso,

Martinelli, Galli-Curci, Ruffo and Melba, among others. He had resigned after a violent battle with Gatti-Casazza, the wound of which had never healed. His temper fired by the brandy, the Maestro would wax eloquent on the subject of his former colleague. He would climax his stream of invectives by screaming, *"Stupido! Stupido!"* Thereupon he would get to his feet, throw down his napkin, pick up a fork and wield it violently, building up to a crescendo that sometimes ended with his breaking the glasses on the table in front of him. They would crash to the floor as he stalked out of the room, a dramatic curtain.

There were many opportunities for me to express to him personally my keen appreciation of his inimitable performances. I recall especially his pleased reaction to my understanding and gratitude for his illumination of the profoundly difficult score of Beethoven's "Missa Solemnis." After his performance, I went backstage and, observing the baton on his dressing table with which he had just conducted the Beethoven masterpiece, I cautiously asked if I might examine it. He handed me the thin mahogany stick, which was about one and half feet long and tapered at the end. "If it could only speak," I mused, fondling it as if it were a magic wand, "what secret messages of joy it would unfold." The Maestro turned to me with his most ingratiating smile and said, "Would you like to keep it?" Until today it is among my small collection of treasured souvenirs.

Occasionally, the Maestro would invite me to hear a segment of a concert with him. We would stand in the rear of the hall to avoid being seen, and afterwards, as we walked back to his apartment together, he would indicate the difference of tempi he would have taken in the piece we had just heard, gesticulating as though he were on the podium. I treasure the memory of one occasion, when he acknowledged to his son-in-law, Vladimir Horowitz, his clear awareness of my unique understanding of the quality of his music-making. As an older man of supreme accomplishment, his affection and regard acted as a spur for me in my own fields of endeavor towards the same lofty standards he so relentlessly pursued. On occasion his confidential relationship with me succeeded in breaking through his almost hermetically sealed isolation. I recall his impromptu visit with his wife, Carla, to my office at Saks Fifth Avenue. He was so entranced by the unexpected break in his routine that he failed to notice that his unexpected appearance had nearly brought the entire organization to a momentary halt.

One summer, while visiting the Salzburg Music Festival in Austria, I took time off to find a source of skiing equipment and apparel for Saks Fifth Avenue. Toscanini was conducting the opera at Salzburg, and one afternoon he and his wife invited me for luncheon at a home in the suburbs. When I announced later that I was going to the city to purchase ski equipment, the Maestro offered to join me. I was delighted when he bounced into the front seat of his car and ordered the chauffeur to rush as at his usual speed of eighty miles per hour to the Lanz store in the center of Salzburg. The Maestro followed me into the store so delighted by his unaccustomed participation in the world of business that he was oblivious to the crowd which had gathered outside to stare at him. Quickly realizing that the prices quoted were minimal, I asked in an offhand manner, "How much for the whole store, and the use of your name?"

When the deal was concluded by a solemn handshake with Lanz, Toscanini almost jumped with childish glee. He drove off in a buoyant mood as though he had just conducted a major performance of one of his beloved Verdi operas.

Toscanini had a truly patrician personality. His raised baton was always an imperious signal to his players, but musicians all agree that the Maestro achieved quicker and greater results from his communication and the clarity of his beat than did any other conductor.

This was captured most uniquely in his re-creation of the Verdi opera masterpieces, many of which he had learned at the feet of the composer. To have heard the music of *La Traviata, Otello* and *Falstaff* rehearsed and then brought to life by Toscanini in performance, is a privileged memory.

It has always baffled me how a conductor standing on a podium directly in front of a hundred players can be aware of how the total confluence of sound is heard in the various sections of the large hall behind him. I especially recall the time during a rehearsal of Schubert's "Unfinished Symphony" in B-flat which I attended, when Toscanini paid me the high compliment of asking me to go up to the balcony and listen to the woodwinds in the second movement and report to him if they were not overpowering the strings. After the rehearsal, as we walked back to his apartment, he told me that until then, in his sixty-eighth year, he had hesitated to approach this Schubert masterpiece. He said that it had always seemed beyond his reach spiritually, requiring the most sensitive balance to weave together the rhythms and the elusive threads of the piece.

Here was the peerless master of the orchestra in obeisance before one of the standard concert pieces that no other conductor hesitates to lead. As we walked he poured out his feelings about the cavalier approach of most conductors to this piece of music which challenged his utmost capacity to penetrate and perform.

"No other conductor hesitates to play this Schubert," he emphasized, "which to me is like a mountaintop that I cannot quite reach. A conductor is born, not made," he concluded. Perhaps one clue to the Maestro's greatness can be found in his humility before the sublime meaning of the scores that he felt privileged to interpret.

Arturo Toscanini became the dominant figure in the world of conducting in the twentieth century. His manner of conducting marked the final transition from the Wagnerian style of over-interpreting to today's more objective approach. To him, interpretation was to be found in only one place, the music. His constant search for the composer's meaning and intention to the letter, along with the uncanny sonority and rhythm he was able to evoke, brought his orchestral players and audiences into a complete involvement with the music.

The Founding of the NBC Symphony Orchestra

To this day, it still seems incredible that the adoring music public was kept in complete ignorance of the fact that their idol, Arturo Toscanini, the world's most eminent conductor, had been dismissed from his post as Music Director of the New York Philharmonic Orchestra in 1936.

But the Maestro's absence from the American scene was to be of short duration. The practical vision of a great corporate executive combined with the love and loyalty of a few friends soon lured him back. In 1937 he returned to the United States to direct an orchestra that had been created and built just for him.

It had begun innocently at a dinner party at the home of Samuel Chotzinoff and his wife, Pauline, the sister of Jascha Heifetz. "Chotzy," who had been the music critic of *The New York World* and *The Post*, literally worshipped the Maestro. Among those at the dinner was David Sarnoff, who headed RCA, which controlled NBC. The dinner conversation had turned to memories of great opera performances, which led to Sarnoff's question, "Whatever became of the Maestro?"

"He is sitting in Italy playing the cello," Chotzy replied sadly. Picking up the cue, I indicated that this was the result of the chicanery of Arthur Judson, whose management company wielded control over most of the conductors in America. In doing so I made certain to include the fact that Judson, as manager of the Philharmonic, had placed the orchestra under the aegis of the fledgling CBS, which under the guidance of its president William S. Paley was beginning to threaten the supremacy of Sarnoff's NBC.

"There must be some way to bring him back," Sarnoff interceded, and the conversation turned to other matters. But Sarnoff, the irrepressible adventurous pioneer in the field of communications, had apparently seen an opportunity to upstage CBS by capturing the world's most celebrated conductor, which would be a coup for NBC. Sarnoff began secretly to contrive ways and means to induce Toscanini to return to America. His first move was to offer Chotzinoff a job at NBC, where at first Chotzy's duties were nebulous. Then Sarnoff revealed that he planned to utilize Chotzy's friendship with the Maestro to bring him back to the United States. Sarnoff was prepared to use the powerful auspices of NBC to build a new symphony orchestra especially for Toscanini, and empowered Chotzy to send a cable to the Maestro at his home in Milan, containing that inducement. As a minor co-conspirator, Chotzy kept me informed of developments. In a few days a cabled reply came from the Maestro. It said succinctly:

"Think to my age. Toscanini."

Saddened by what seemed to him a polite refusal, Chotzy took the cable to Sarnoff, who reacted by saying, "This is great. He didn't say no." Sarnoff then asked who had the greatest personal influence with the Maestro and was told it was Chotzy's wife, Pauline. He immediately commissioned the Chotzinoffs to embark on a ship and go to Italy, taking with them a contract prepared for Toscanini's signature.

The full story of how the Chotzinoffs prevailed upon the Maestro is an epic in itself. Only the persistence of devoted, trusted friends could have possibly broken down the resistance of this proud Italian patrician who felt he had been shamefully demeaned by the insensitive Board of the New York Philharmonic.

The American music world owes a priceless debt of gratitude to the Chotzinoffs. After three weeks of patient maneuvering and quiet pressure, the Maestro assented and signed the contract that Chotzinoff had brought with him. It contained a clause which stated that NBC would build a symphony orchestra exclusively for the Maestro, and composed of the finest musicians available and subject to his approval.

It was a prodigious musical enterprise. Leading musicians from all corners of the world were gathered to form the new orchestra, which was prepared and rehearsed by Artur Rodzinski, who at one time had been the conductor of the Philharmonic and whose technical skill would satisfy the impeccable standards of the Maestro in advance of his arrival. Only an organization with the enormous financial resources of RCA and the sensitive, guiding hand of Samuel Chotzinoff could have achieved it.

The first performance of the NBC Symphony Orchestra under Toscanini took place on Christmas night in 1937. Under the Maestro's baton the NBC Symphony became one of the world's premier orchestras. For seventeen seasons its sterling performances reached into millions of American homes through the NBC radio network.

During Toscanini's opening performance as conductor of the new NBC Symphony Orchestra, I sat with Sarnoff and Chotzy and could not resist a moment of nostalgia. I recalled the casual conversation at the informal dinner party only eight months back when a chance question regarding the Maestro's whereabouts had sparked a concept out of which a monumental musical achievement had materialized.

Performances of the NBC Symphony Orchestra were broadcast live from Studio 8-H in the NBC building at Rockefeller Center. Attendance was limited to a few hundred invited guests, as the small hall permitted only a privileged few to hear and see the Maestro in command of his orchestra at close range. For me the musical impact of those incredible performances heard in such an intimate setting has never been surpassed. For the following seventeen years, audiences, whose numbers were in the millions, were fortunate to be able to enjoy the Maestro's peerless performances on the radio in their homes. In addition, Toscanini has bequeathed us a heritage of matchless music-making through his many recordings on the RCA label, which belong today among the world's timeless music treasures.

The Origin of the Palestine (Israel) Symphony Orchestra

In the 1930s many of the first-rate orchestra players who were forced to leave the leading German and Austrian symphonies because they were Jews, spilled into Palestine. Bronislaw Hubermann, a violin soloist and one of Germany's celebrated personalities, was among those who found haven in Palestine. He seized the opportunity to collect the evicted players and form a new local symphony orchestra.

I first met Hubermann when he came to America to perform Beethoven sonatas with his colleague, Artur Schnabel. Later I was inspired when I heard of his plan to form a Palestine Symphony Orchestra.

In New York I attended a meeting convened to discuss generating support for this project and to set up a sponsoring committee. Someone suggested that if we could induce Arturo Toscanini to lend his name to the list of those on this committee it would be a coup and add inestimable prestige to the fledgling symphony. I volunteered to approach my friend, the Maestro, and suggested that Hubermann accompany me. I knew that the Maestro was aware of Hubermann's unique artistry, as I had attended one of the artist's concerts with him at Town Hall. After the concert we had walked back together to the Maestro's apartment in the Hotel Astor and had discussed the quality of Hubermann's performance.

Hubermann had for many years been one of the musical darlings of Germany. A vibrant personality with a powerful intellect, he had wielded a strong influence in European artistic circles. Not the handsomest of men, his appearance was further marred by his decidedly crossed eyes. It was a cruel joke among musicians that his affliction was caused by his keeping one eye on his violin, and the other on the box office while on stage.

The Maestro, always the soul of charm, received us graciously in the small drawing room of his apartment. Hubermann, sitting on a couch opposite the Maestro, carefully outlined his plan. I watched the Maestro as he listened attentively, and noticed that his eyes had fastened on Hubermann's trouser legs. Following his eyes I noticed that Hubermann's European-style pants narrowed slightly and ended a good four inches above his ankles. He concluded his presentation with a list of those celebrities who had agreed to sponsor the inaugural concert to be held the following spring, and then began haltingly to propose to Toscanini that "it would be wonderful, Maestro, if we could count on you." Before he could finish his sentence the Maestro interrupted and said, "Fine, I will conduct the first concert." He then stood up abruptly, shook hands with Hubermann, who made some sputtering efforts at "thanks," led him to the door, bade him good-bye and asked me to stay.

As soon as the door had closed behind Hubermann, the Maestro called his wife Carla, who was in the next room. He then began pacing the room, repeating, *"Che pantalone! Che pantalone!"* pointing to the couch on which Hubermann had sat. He then exploded in Italian that in all his born days he had never seen such strange, ill-fitting trousers, exhorting me to explain how such an eminent violinist could wear such terrible-fitting trousers. The Maestro was impeccable in the fit and unobtrusiveness of his clothes, and apparently a sartorial off beat could offend his sensibilities as much as an orchestral one could offend his musical taste. At tea, the Maestro's spontaneous offer to conduct the first concert of the newly formed orchestra was not even discussed.

The next spring the Palestine Symphony Orchestra was inaugurated in Jerusalem. Arturo Toscanini was its first conductor. Since 1948, when it became the Israel Symphony Orchestra, it has taken its place among the world's leading symphonic bodies. There is hardly a single leading conductor or soloist who has not performed with this illustrious orchestra, truly a jewel in Israel's crown.

Dorme Bene, Caro

In the summer of 1933 I was sent to the London Economic Conference to make a confidential report to Professor Felix Frankfurter, a close advisor to the newly elected President, Franklin D. Roosevelt. After the Conference I headed for the sunnier shores of Lake Como, Italy, where Artur Schnabel had moved from Berlin.

Looking back, it seems strange that Italy under Mussolini's dominance should have become a haven for many of the German and Austrian artists fleeing Fascism when Toscanini, a national hero in Italy, had recently been attacked by street gangs in Bologna for refusing to play the Fascist national hymn, "The Giovenezza." However, there had not yet been any evidence of repression against foreign artists.

The Schnabel villa overlooking the blue waters of Lake Como became a sanctuary for such leading artists as Otto Klemperer, Paul Hindemith, George Szell, and many others. While there I received a telegram from Toscanini inviting me to visit him at his retreat in Isola Bella at Lake Maggiore. Arriving from Milan to nearby Pallanza, I was met by a small motor boat and whisked to the magical island. The Maestro was at the pier to meet me, a beret on his head at a perky angle but otherwise dressed in his usual morning costume: gray striped trousers, black alpaca coat, bow tie and soft slippers. He greeted me with his infectious smile and guided me along the gently curving, flower-lined path that led to his modest villa. As we walked, he fairly pirouetted, turning this way and that to point out the exquisite views from his glorious island.

After we had had what seemed to me a gargantuan midday meal with his wife Carla and a few of her elderly friends, at which the Maestro had as always eaten sparingly, he and I sauntered from the table to the piazza. He was then in his late sixties and loved to boast of his physical powers. Sleep, he used to say, was a waste of time. "Only women need to sleep," he had once confided to me slyly.

"Are you accustomed to taking a nap after lunch?" the Maestro inquired, peering closely at me through his thick glasses.

I hesitated for a moment before answering. This was probably the Maestro's polite way of excusing himself before going off for his own siesta.

"Yes," I finally sputtered, though in all my memory I had never before taken a nap in the afternoon.

"*Bene,*" snapped the Maestro, "I never do. I do not need sleep. I will show you to your room."

Caught flat-footed, I followed him sadly up the winding stairs, feeling like a child being sent to bed. The Maestro raced ahead of me, taking the stairs two at a time. He opened the door quietly on a room that looked out on the lake. It was a dream view. He went to the window, pulled the old-fashioned shutters together, closing them carefully to shut out the afternoon sun. Then, going over to the bed, he pressed his fingers down into the mattress, testing its softness. Satisfied, he smiled at me affectionately, tiptoed to the door, opened it gently, then turned to me and said, *"Dorme bene, caro"* (Sleep well, my dear). I could hear his soft, measured tread as he descended the stairs.

There was nothing left for me to do but lie down. So I took off my shoes, stretched out on the bed, folded my hands behind my head and stared up at the ceiling. Never had I felt more awake!

After about ten minutes of immobility, during which I reflected on my host's gentleness and infinite consideration, I suddenly noticed that the house had become very still. The sounds of conversation from the ladies on the piazza below, which had been drifting upwards, had stopped. The strains from a few chords on the piano in the Maestro's study below, where he was preparing for a Brahms cycle with the New York Philharmonic, had also ceased.

Restless and impatient, I got up, walked to the bedroom door and peered down the hall. Almost without realizing it, on impulse I went tiptoeing down the broad encircling stairs in my stockinged feet. The utter quiet, the absence of any sound or life, gave me courage to descend all the way. As I reached the bottom of the stairs, my heart began to beat faster. Suppose I was caught? How could I explain? Still hesitant, I ventured a few steps into the hall toward the Maestro's study. Seeing the door open and hearing no sound, I tiptoed nearer until I reached the door. By this time I was feeling like a truant child, but my mounting curiosity overcame my feeling of guilt, and I peered into the room. There at the piano sat the Maestro, score in front of him, head down on the keys. He was fast asleep.

Chapter Four

Artur Schnabel—Enduring Personality

Meeting Schnabel and Hitler in Berlin

An accidental meeting in the piano department of the Bamberger Department Store resulted in propelling me all the way from Newark, New Jersey to Berlin, Germany in 1932.

During my busy days as Advertising Director of Bamberger's, I discovered that the piano department offered a haven to which I could retreat. Pianos have always fascinated me, and seeing so many in one place was an abundance of riches and an invitation for frequent visits. Occasionally, when there were no customers around to interfere, I would sneak in an impromptu practice session at a piano. On one visit, I noticed a well-known local music teacher, Mrs. Clara Husserl, seated at one of the grands helping a student select a piano. At that moment it occurred to me that Bamberger's piano department could become a center of Newark's musical activities. So were born the Bamberger Music Scholarships which annually enabled ten gifted young New Jerseyites to study for a year at the Institute of Musical Art (now the Julliard School of Music) in New York. Winners of these scholarships were selected by a panel of distinguished judges after a series of eliminations. The program identified the Bamberger name with leading musicians and educators and resulted in much favorable publicity for the store. It was an early application of my format of blending music with a practical business activity.

Mrs. Husserl greeted me warmly and took the opportunity to mention that her daughter, Hortense Monath, a brilliant young pianist, had just returned from a successful concert tour in Europe. To enlist my help in furthering her daughter's career in this country, a dinner party was arranged for me to meet her, which I reluctantly agreed to attend.

I was seated next to Hortense at the dinner, which I recall as one of those obligation affairs. Hortense, who was then the wife of a wealthy Viennese businessman, was irresistibly attractive, with dark eyes, severely swept-back black hair and striking ivory skin. At the dinner she made no effort to conceal her low opinion of most Americans' superficial approach to serious music.

Toward the end of the dinner, to make conversation, I remarked that on the previous evening I had heard an incredible concert of the two Brahms piano concerti played by the Boston Symphony Orchestra under Serge Koussevitsky, and that I had been especially deeply impressed by the soloist, Artur Schnabel, whose unique articulation and command of the piano had been a revelation to me. Hortense's reaction was one of startled excitement. She revealed that she literally worshipped Schnabel and had been the first American pianist to study with him in Berlin. In fact, she planned to return to Germany that summer to continue her studies with Schnabel, whose students included many of the world's most distinguished young pianists.

I invited Hortense to attend a concert of the Philharmonic Orchestra at Carnegie Hall the following Thursday evening. There, during the intermission I introduced her to Arthur Judson. He invited us to join him in his box for the balance of the concert. The meeting helped open the door to her American concert career. From this beginning, my friendship with Hortense (who later became my wife), grew and deepened, so that when she left for Europe in July, I followed her to Berlin, where she introduced me to Artur Schnabel and arranged for me to have the rare privilege of attending one of his classes. That evening the session included some of the most illustrious future pianists, and the lesson opened up new musical horizons for me. In my mind's eye I can still clearly see the studio in Schnabel's home at Wielandstrasse 14, Kurfürstendamm, Berlin, where Schnabel and his wife Therese, one of Germany's celebrated lieder singers, held musical court.

In the center of the long, rectangular studio, there were two grand pianos. About a dozen students were seated either on chairs or on the floor in a circle around the pianos. At a signal from Schnabel, one of the students would get up, go over to a piano, and play a major work without interruption. Schnabel sat at the other piano or walked quietly around the room during the performance, puffing on a heavy black cigar. When the piece was over, he began a broad discussion of the structure and background of the music. To illustrate some passage, he often sang it in his deep bass voice. He employed numerous devices to communicate his ideas on the inner meaning of the music to the students, sometimes even impromptu poetry. Small in stature, with gray hair brushed severely back, his luminous steel-gray eyes would seem almost to drill through his pupil and then the next moment switch to pools of tenderness. That evening marked the beginning of my awareness of the Schnabel genius.

The lesson ended at midnight. Afterwards, electrified by the experience, I sat up in my hotel room until the early hours of the morning writing an analysis of Schnabel's magnetic personality and his articulate communication with his students. I still possess the outline that I wrote that night and in retrospect can see how futile it was to attempt to capture in words the secret of Schnabel's mysterious gift for conveying the very heart of the music's meaning to his students. Next morning, I showed my outline to Hortense who insisted that Schnabel should see it and arranged for me to meet with him privately. He expressed a polite interest in my outline, but pointed out that the written word could not possibly communicate the underlying spirit of the music. He explained that his reason for teaching with a second piano was that it was only through the music itself that he was able to illustrate his ideas.

Having previously learned of Schnabel's interest in politics, I took advantage of the meeting to introduce some questions about the boiling unrest I had observed in Germany. This touched a responsive chord and led him to dwell exhaustively on his growing concern about Germany's rapid transition to a new and diabolical militarism from the rise of the Nazi movement, which was sweeping through the country with an increasing momentum. He urged me to do what I could when I returned to the United States to awaken the American people to the peril of the growing menace of Adolf Hitler.

In spite of the brevity of our meeting, his amiability and warmth communicated a feeling of personal interest in me that was to develop into an expanding bond of friendship during his visit to the United States the following year.

Schnabel's warning took on greater meaning for me two days after our meeting. While walking through the streets of Berlin I was attracted by the sight of a crowd gathered to attend what seemed to be a rabble-rousing political meeting. Curiosity prompted me to move toward the meeting and to hear the message of the speaker, whose voice had risen to an hysterical tirade. At a distance, the speaker with his small, clipped mustache reminded me momentarily of Charlie Chaplin. I asked for the name of the speaker who held such a grip on his audience and was told it was Adolf Hitler. Though my German was rudimentary, I was able to follow and understand the cascade of threats which poured from him.

"When I am Chancellor of Germany," erupted from him in a shrill falsetto, "the first thing I will do is to kill all the Jews, all of them, first in Germany and then throughout the world."

Stunned by Hitler's apocalyptic words, I was even more disturbed by the response of his listeners, who applauded him almost ecstatically.

"He is talking about *me*," I kept repeating to myself as I gradually retreated to the edge of the crowd. I wandered through the streets of Berlin that night, my mind churning with new thoughts that Adolf Hitler had aroused in me. It had taken this political maniac to jolt me into an awareness of my Jewish identity.

During my six-day voyage back home on the massive German liner, the S.S. Europa, I heard more offensive Nazi talk and wrote down my impressions of my visit in Germany, ending with the prediction that if nothing was done to stop Hitler in his tracks, he and his Nazi horde would soon take over Germany and eventually all of Europe.

When the Europa docked in New York I was interviewed by reporters and released a written statement. The next day I received a phone call from a friend, Adolph Ochs, then publisher of *The New York Times*. He gently admonished me for my "emotional overreaction" to Hitler's threats but said that he was obliged to print my story as it was "news."

I had sent a cable to WOR from the ship with instructions to reserve a key time spot for me to make an important statement about Germany. Two important men aroused by my broadcast were Morris L. Ernst, the famed attorney, and Ernest Gruening, then editor of *The Nation*, (later Governor of and Senator from Alaska). They phoned me at the station and invited me to join them at the "21 Club" in New York. There they grilled me about my findings in Germany, and Gruening asked for my permission to publish the script of my radio broadcast in *The Nation*. In addition he invited me to accompany him to a dinner the following evening at the home of a friend. The friend turned out to be Fiorello La Guardia. When we arrived at his home, a modest apartment on the unfashionable upper area of Fifth Avenue, we found a group of men sitting around a table in their shirt sleeves. Among them were Adolph Berle, Sidney Hillman and Newbold Morris. During dinner, which consisted of pasta fagiola, an Italian dish that was new to me, they continued to plan the strategy for the campaign to elect La Guardia Mayor of New York and wrest the power from the corrupt hands of Tammany Hall, which had brought New York to the brink of bankruptcy. My impromptu suggestions during the dinner resulted in La Guardia inviting me to take an active part in his campaign, which was my baptism into politics. More important, it served as the beginning of a close friendship, which lasted through La Guardia's lifetime. In addition to our common zeal for honest government, I learned that we also shared a passion for good music. In fact, some of the strategy for his mayoralty campaign was reviewed during the intermissions of concerts we attended together at Carnegie Hall, sitting in the upper balcony.

Meanwhile, my unrelenting efforts to sound an alert about the perils ahead from a Nazi takeover in Germany had met with little success. In fact, my efforts to picture the dire consequences for America only brought me into conflict with a number of leading citizens who simply dismissed Hitler as a raucous aberration.

In my desperate efforts to arouse the leadership of the American-Jewish community to the imminent danger facing the Jews of Europe, I turned to Felix Frankfurter. He was then a professor at the Harvard Law School and a close advisor to President Roosevelt, who later appointed him to the Supreme Court. Frankfurter, too, was appalled at the passivity of most leading American Jews in light of the oncoming crisis. He suggested that I might be more successful if I would work within the framework of the traditional Jewish organizations. When I continued to insist that I believed I would be more effective working as an individual, he arranged for me to see Justice Louis Brandeis, saying, "Brandeis is a great man; perhaps he can convince you where I apparently cannot."

I received a letter from Brandeis, written in his own hand, inviting me to come to see him in his home in Washington on the following Saturday.

The Justice, who in profile bore a striking resemblance to Abraham Lincoln, received me in his study, which was almost ascetic in its spareness. He told me he had been born in Kentucky and had become a Zionist late in life and was now convinced that "until the Jewish people have a homeland they will always be the first victims of tyranny and oppression."

One of the gems of wisdom the great man shared with me came in reply to my query, "Why do people fear making an unpopular decision, why do they lack individual courage?"

"People do not avoid making such decisions out of fear," he replied. "It is the inconvenience that deters them."

When I asked him why so many people, especially Jews, remained blind and complacent in the light of the palpable and transparent threats from Hitler, he told me, "They just don't know any better. In my eighty years of life I have learned one thing: Human judgment at best is bad."

My face-to-face talk with this noble personality left an impression on me that has not been lost to this day. While he did not convince me to join any regular Zionist organization, he did inspire me to intensify my efforts to awaken our people to the growing peril from Hitler, with all the means at my disposal.

Brandeis's philosophical ideas helped explain the attitude of the influential Jewish leaders but did nothing to move them out of their passive indifference. They continued to avert their eyes from the fast approaching danger of Nazism and to ignore the creeping menace facing European Jewry, which had been singled out by Hitler as his prime target.

The fates that had contrived to bring about my meeting with Hortense through our common love of music became the pivot on which the entire course of my future life turned. Her musical gifts and attractiveness as a woman drew me to follow her to Berlin, where I met two men who changed the direction of my life.

Hearing Adolf Hitler personally pronouncing the death sentence he was preparing for the Jewish people, propelled me into an active concern for their welfare which continues to this very day.

Artur Schnabel, the great man who lifted my sights to a broader understanding of music's exalted meaning, was to become my cherished friend. Today, his spirit remains alive through his music, while Hitler and his legions are all dead.

Legend and Legacy

In 1932, Artur Schnabel's unique personality and consummate musicianship had already won him primacy among European concert artists, and his fame even then had begun to spread to the United States. When I was given the rare privilege of sitting in on some of his master classes to observe him, he worked with such artists as Clifford Curzon, Rudolf Firkusny, Betty Humby, Leon Fleisher, Lilli Kraus and Hortense Monath, all of whom became, along with Claude Frank, Schnabel's last pupil, the leading interpreters of piano literature of our day.

Schnabel transferred his home and classes from Berlin to Lake Como in 1933, when Hitler's threats and the rise of the Nazi movement made life in Germany unendurable. His classes were unique in that each of the students was already a recognized artist in his or her own right. Each student was invited to attend the two- to three-hour lessons of all the others, and as a result they all benefited by learning the scores of all the music the group was working on. For each performer it was a grueling test to play while surrounded by colleagues—in effect by a jury of peers. But all grudgingly admitted that it was an invaluable experience. Technique and the mechanics of playing were taken for granted. In these master classes Schnabel was concerned only with conveying the inner spirit of the music and in searching for the original intention of the composer.

Former students of Schnabel say that he could illustrate anything on the second piano; that he had studied and memorized virtually the entire literature; that his technique was staggering.

He often used word imagery or coined phrases in which the rhyme scheme matched the musical phrase. I recall hearing him remark one time that the rhapsodic passage for solo piano in the slow movement of Brahms's B-flat Concerto should be "streaming, not dreaming"; and when savoring a particular harmony, "It is like a rare wine on the tongue." I can remember his contrasting of composers by saying, "Mozart is a garden; Schubert a forest; Beethoven is a mountain range." The totality of this, the music, the unbridled enthusiasm, often a performance by Schnabel himself at the second piano along with those of his talented students, made each session an electrifying experience which left the students spent and ecstatic.

Schnabel was a man of marked originality. His eminence as a musician and a teacher was enhanced by his striking personality and superbly analytical mind. In appearance he was short and stocky, with piercing steel-gray eyes and white hair severely brushed back. His brilliantly articulate discourses on world affairs were no less commanding than his release of the purity of the music of a Mozart sonata at the piano.

A *wunderkind*, at the age of twelve Schnabel was already so accomplished a musician that he was sent from his home in Lipnik, Austria to Vienna* to study with the illustrious teacher Theodor Leschetizky. Legend has it that once, during a lesson, Leschetizky called out to his young pupil: "You will never be a pianist, you are a musician." As we know, Schnabel was indeed a great musician, but he was also one the world's finest pianists. Schnabel took special delight in repeating Leschetizky's prophecy which he considered a paradox, for to him the pianist and the musician were completely fused, though the pianist always remained the servant of the musician.

When Schnabel was in Vienna at the turn of the twentieth century, Brahms was the great idol of Europe's musical world. Young Schnabel, however, with the perverse independence which was one of his chief characteristics, refused to join in the general worship of the heavily bearded German master. Finally, one day Leschetizky turned to Schnabel and said: "Schubert wrote a number of sonatas for the piano which no one ever plays. Here are several; you may like them."

In Schnabel's own words: "In them I found a full supply of happiness." Among them was Schubert's posthumous B-flat sonata, which after hearing Schnabel perform it, became for me akin to a declaration of love. I later studied this sonata, first with Schnabel's son, Karl Ulrich, and later with Claude Frank. To this day I continue my unending search to realize its heavenly discourse at the piano.

Schnabel's performances of Schubert's heretofore unknown master-

---

* In Vienna, then at the height of its musical supremacy, the young Schnabel had a young medical student to assist him with his academic studies. He was Dr. Siegfried Husserl, who later emigrated to Newark, New Jersey. His daughter, Hortense, became my wife.

pieces became a hallmark of his legendary greatness. His public acclaim grew steadily in European capitals. He first gained recognition when he organized the Schnabel Trio, which included Pablo Casals and Carl Flesch. But his fame flared across Europe following his spectacular performances of all of Beethoven's thirty-two piano sonatas. These were presented in non-chronological order in a cycle of consecutive concerts first in Berlin, and then in Vienna and London. In 1936, he repeated this mammoth cycle in New York to crowded audiences at Carnegie Hall.

When Schnabel arrived in New York, I invited two musical friends, Richard Simon and Max Schuster, to meet him. The two partners in a then-fledgling publishing business were completely captured by his charm and erudition.

Schnabel had just completed writing a treatise on his musical philosophy, *Reflections on Music.* They immediately volunteered to publish it, and I was given the privilege of editing it and writing the introduction. It appeared in a uniquely bound, beautifully designed limited edition. A masterpiece of abstract treatment of music from the beginning of simple sound to the ultimate Beethoven C-sharp Minor Quartet, it is today a collector's piece. Later, I suggested to Richard Simon and Max Schubert that they also publish the Schnabel edition of Beethoven's thirty-two piano sonatas. Today that edition is universally recognized to be the definitive interpretation of the Beethoven masterworks. It is used by pianists and students the world over, who are the beneficiaries of Schnabel's profound scholarship. Of special value are the interpretations in the many footnotes in German, French and English which accompany most of the scores.

In 1942 I suggested to Schnabel that he repeat his cycle of performances of the thirty-two Beethoven sonatas for the New Friends of Music concerts. He demurred, explaining that to do so he would have to practice, which he was disinclined to do.

"What about all of Schubert's piano works?" he countered. I could hardly believe my ears and accepted his offer with alacrity. There is no record that such a comprehensive performance of the vast Schubert piano literature in one continuous cycle of concert had ever before been attempted.

Schnabel's five consecutive concerts of Schubert's piano music for the New Friends of Music constituted a landmark contribution to the art of the piano. The vast and varied piano works of Schubert comprise fifteen major sonatas, sixteen fantasies, numerous impromptus and other solo pieces, and thirty-one waltzes and dances; these in addition to his prolific output of over 600 exquisite lieder, his symphonic works and his chamber music, which was then only sporadically played and scarcely appreciated.

Many great pianists have their luminous day in the sun and then gradually fade from memory. The examples of Paderewski, Josef Hofmann and Harold Bauer come to mind. Not so with Schnabel, whose influence increases with the years. His many pupils carry on with his unimpeachable standards. His recordings of the thirty-two Beethoven sonatas was a feat which took him from 1931 to 1935 to complete. There was a quality of disembodiment and self-effacement in his playing that left us to deal with the music only, as though there had been no intermediary.

Behind his performances were an incomparable style, intellectual strength, and phrasing of such aristocratic purity it carried his listeners to an exalted level. His fierce integrity, brilliant mind and incisive tongue made him one of the most respected musicians of the century.

Schnabel belongs to the future. He died thirty years ago; yet more of his records are sold today than during his lifetime. Then his style of playing was attacked; now it has been accepted and adopted by the leading pianists of today. They can hardly believe that the ideas which he introduced were in his lifetime considered revolutionary or that he had to fight for what is now completely accepted. He fought for the correct rendition of the composer's text and was called schoolmasterly; today, anyone who does not follow a score faithfully is blamed for misrepresentation. He fought for better con-cert programs and was told they would drive audiences away. But his con-

cept of programs concentrating on a single composer has had a healthy influence on today's program-making, although, regrettably, most programs
are still "mixed," a hangover from tradition and from the desire on the part
of performers to please everyone, which ends by pleasing no one, including the critics.

From the moment that I met this magnetic personality in his study in Berlin,
I sensed that an affinity would grow between us, though I was almost three
decades his junior. How could I expect, however, that the spark that struck acci-
dentally during that crucial visit to Germany would flame into a friendship so
secure and enduring as to become one of the most profound experiences in my
life, my personal philosophy, my musical insight, and even in public affairs? One
of the many pungent aphorisms he loved to make to students at the piano,
"Immer weiter" (Ever forward), has served as a compass for my life's direction.

Schnabel left his home in Germany in 1933 following the cancellation of his
participation in a Brahms Festival because he was Jewish. When Furtwängler
begged him to return and play with him in Germany, Schnabel's answer was
typical and unambiguous.

"Not until every Jewish artist and every Jewish orchestra player is welcome in Germany."

In 1936 he was living in the United States and was a spiritual and strate-
gic backbone to me in my successful campaign to force the Board of Directors
of the New York Philharmonic to withdraw its invitation to Furtwängler to
succeed Toscanini as Music Director of the orchestra.

Part of the root of our friendship was that we both drew inspiration from the
countryside; the trees, flowers, sky and mountain peaks. Perhaps the most
memorable steps he and I enjoyed together were taken during our "climbs."
They began in Sils Maria, Switzerland, and during the war were transferred
to Colorado. These were not perilous, but slow, manageable rock-climbs.
After some foot slipping and torturous turns, we would pause in some idyl-

Fiorello La Guardia, Ira Hirschmann, Arturo Toscanini. New York. 1938.

Composer Arnold Schoenberg with Fritz Stiedry, conductor
of the New Friends orchestra, and Ira Hirschmann.

ARNOLD SCHOENBERG
116 N. ROCKINGHAM AVE.
BRENTWOOD PARK
LOS ANGELES, CALIF.
TEL. W.L.A. 35077

Mr.Ira Hirschmann
care of New Friends of Music,Inc.
15 West   44th Street
New York   December 8,1940

Dear Mr.Hirschmann:

          I feel I owe you this letter in which
I am going to tell you my great appreciation for
the a/chievments of the society you have created,
the New Friends of Music.

          Really:this is something which should be
a model to all places of culture or such which
want to be considered as such.

          Such a group of young and fiery people,
who are really devoted to music as an art and who
alone,therefore are able to influence,convince and
conquerenemjes,weaklings and dullwitted people;
such apowerfull group of idealists,of fighters,
of believers — that is the group which is able to
create culture,to promote the arts,to be increase
the values of life.

          May I tell you,that(beyond my own interest
in performing a new work of mine,which you also
commissioned)I thank you even more for the foun-
dation of this society whose great merits are already bearing fruits at present,but will bear more
in future.

          Mr.Stiedry asked me to assure you that
in case I would add more movements to this Chamber
Symphony,I would consider them as a part of our
contract and as belonging to the rights which I
have given to the New Friends of Music.But again
I can assure that this work will not be extended —
not by me:because it is not an Unfinished(chamber)
Symphony.But in case there should grow by itself or
caused through a disease some cancroid reproductions,
and one could call them musical ones,I would not
deny my duty to give you the rights on them—if
you still want them
          With many kind regards and best greetings
to Mrs.Hirschman I am yours
                    most sincerely Arnold Schoenberg

Letter from Arnold Schoenberg to Ira Hirschmann.

Tile of Verdi by Lotte Lehmann.

Maestro Toscanini's personal inscription to Ira Hirschmann
on plate designed by Lotte Lehmann.

Photograph of Toscanini, personally
inscribed to Ira Hirschmann.

Ira Hirschmann and Artur Schnabel.

Hotel Peter Stuyvesant

CENTRAL PARK WEST ○ AT 86TH STREET
8TH AVENUE SUBWAY AT YOUR DOOR

New York

April 3rd, 1942

Dear Hirschmann,

I highly appreciate your
motive for not accepting my small
— extramusical — contribution to the
memorable Art of Fugue presentation
last Sunday. My contribution did
in no way imply a criticism of dis-
positions made for this occasion by the
Friends of Music. I was glad for the
opportunity to "contribute" and you will
do me a favour in allowing me a pleasure
which, if I could, I should love to
enjoy more often,

Heartiest A.S.

CENTRAL PARK — YOUR FRONT LAWN

Letter from Artur Schnabel to Ira Hirschmann.

Conductor Wilhelm Furtwängler on his podium in Berlin bows to
Adolf Hitler (seated in front row).

Otto Klemperer

TELEPHONE, 01-235-2000

TELEGRAMS, HIGHCASTE, LONDON, S.W.1.
TELEX, 262057.

March 15th, 1969.

HYDE PARK HOTEL, KNIGHTSBRIDGE,

LONDON, S.W.1.

Dear Ira Hirschmann,

my son, Werner, who is a few days here in London, brought
the wonderful news that perhaps you will come to my last
"Fidelio" performance on March 24th.

I always hoped to see you once more in this life. Now
there is the possibility. Please do your best to come.
Then we can talk of the past, - also the future, which
is not cheering.

I have not and never will forget all you did for me, when
things were very bad in my life, - so let me hope that
you will come.

Your old friend

Otto Klemperer

Otto Klemperer

Letter from Otto Klemperer to Ira Hirschmann.

Bronze bust of Toscanini donated by
Mayor La Guardia to the original building
of the High School of Music and Art.

Ira Hirschmann and Fiorello La Guardia.

WABF
Statement of Aims:

WRITTEN BY THE FOUNDER AT THE INCEPTION OF THE STATION,
ANNOUNCED TO THE PUBLIC JANUARY 1948

1. To offer the best in the literature of music in all its forms through the modern, faithful broadcasting medium, Frequency Modulation (FM), with emphasis on the piano literature which has suffered distortion and neglect from the limitations imposed by the AM broadcasting method, now becoming obsolete.

2. To conceive programs as units based on a central musical idea, with a proper relationship of one composition to another in key-signature, balance and listening interest and to present, wherever possible, complete cycles of composers' works.

3. To offer all compositions *in their entirety* with no interruptions between movements for any purpose, no excerpts or cutting for "fill in" time or overtime. The vulgar, indiscriminate use of musical excerpts—commonly known as theme songs—extracted from one composition to introduce others, will not be permitted as advertising trade-marks or for any other purpose.

4. To respect the integrity of the music, performing artists and their audience through the use of flexible schedules, eliminating split-second timing and cut-offs and allowing extra time, when necessary, to assure the normal completion of all programs. The clock will always be subordinate to the program.

5. To demonstrate that commercial sponsors can advertise their products effectively in a natural speaking voice, with the standard of dignity and good taste set by the Station *without* jingles, singing commercials, high-pressure selling or exaggerated claims.

6. To reach an ever-growing audience from which the Station can draw its main support through active participation rather than anonymous listening so that the Station can flourish as a useful instrument of the community.

THE NEW FRIENDS OF MUSIC, INC.,
of New York, U.S.A.

Announces a Concert of

CHAMBER MUSIC
OF

WOLFGANG AMADEUS
MOZART

and

Ludwig van BEETHOWEN
Sunday, March 26, 1944
9.30 P. M.

Ankara Palace Hotel

R. S. V. P.
I. A. Hirschmann
American Embassy
Ankara.

Buffet:
10:45 P. M.

PROGRAM

1. String Quartet B. Major, K. 458
   W. A. Mozart

   Allegro vivace assai

   Menuetto

   Adagio

   Allegro assai

2. String Quartet opus 18, No. 6 in B - flat
   Ludwig van Beethoven

   Allegro con brio

   Adagio ma non troppo

   Scherzo

   La Malinconia - Adagio - Allegretto
   quasi allegro.

Please do not applaud between movements

THE QUARTET:

Gilbert Back   I violin

Sedat Ediz   II violin

Izzet Albayrak   Viola

Mesut Cemil   Violoncello

Please bring this program with you.
Doors will be closed at 9.35 P. M.

Program of chamber music concert at a 1944 diplomatic reception in Ankara,
Turkey performed by the "New Friends of Music—Ankara Branch."

lic spot before making the final ascent. When at last we reached the peak and viewed the endless vistas surrounding us, Schnabel would exclaim, "Here and now is when we lose all our egotism!"

Before each climb I would select a composer to be the subject of the day for discussion: Beethoven, Schubert, or Schumann. As he led the way he would answer my questions, unfolding an imagery that matched the magical surroundings. His differentiation of the special genius of each composer was a rare education which, combined with the privileged companionship, lifted me closer to the stars.

What will be the great legacy of Artur Schnabel? Will time exhaust the infinite scope of his mind, heart and articulation? Hardly. Fortunately, Schnabel had bequeathed us an imperishable living legacy both in his recordings and in his editing of the thirty-two Beethoven sonatas. Yet the deepest dedication in his life was not to his performances but to his students, whom he nourished and lifted to a full realization of their musical gifts. For Schnabel, teaching became an article of faith, and it is the new generations of musicians who will carry on the enduring legacy of Artur Schnabel.

My Return to Music

When I left my diplomatic post in Turkey and returned to the United States in 1945, after two years of grueling rescue operations, I found it difficult to reset my roots in the old patterns. My daily responsibilities as vice president of Bloomingdale's, which had formerly absorbed me, could not hold my interest. The problems of retailing seemed far remote from the life-and-death struggles which had occupied my thoughts and energies for so many months.

During my travels through devastated lands, I had contracted malaria, a recurring disease which at times brought on spasms of depression entirely foreign to my normal optimistic outlook. On one lonely evening, when the malaria bug had plunged me into darkness, my eyes were suddenly drawn, as though by a magnet, to the grand piano in the corner of my living room. I approached the instrument gingerly, and hesitantly reached for one of my favorite Schubert Impromptus. As I played, my gloom gradually dissipated, and the room seemed to come aglow. The Schubert under my own fingers had apparently communicated a timely message: that what I needed was the nourishment of music. I decided to take up my piano studies again.

During the years of my marriage, my wife Hortense had occupied the musical throne in our home. I had gladly let my amateur music studies take second place to her long hours of daily practicing for her public performances. During my long absence from the country I had abandoned my piano studies, but now, as I contemplated pouring myself into the study of some Beethoven sonatas, my spirits began to revive.

I wrote to my friend and confidant Artur Schnabel and asked him to recommend a piano teacher for me. Schnabel replied immediately with a letter that was an inspirational lifeline.

"Don't every worry about yourself," he wrote. "In your momentary descent you have turned to the highest mountain, your music. May I have the privilege of being your teacher?"

Thus, with the incomparable musical and spiritual guidance of the great man, and regular lessons with his son, Karl Ulrich, I began my slow climb up a new road.

Over the years my two- to three-hour sessions with Karl Ulrich added a new dimension to my musical insight at the piano. The inexpressible joy I had discovered from hearing and sharing the outpouring of music masterpieces became a highly recreative experience which I was now probing to its depths.

I owe a priceless debt to Karl Ulrich for reconstructing my piano technique, which facilitated my capacity for articulation by simply the use of my hands and fingers in the approach to the piano. I was the beneficiary of the unique musical gifts Karl had inherited from his celebrated father and particularly from his mother, who as Theresa Baer had been Europe's foremost lieder singer. Karl loved to tell of the endless hours he had spent as a boy in Berlin learning the piano parts, equal companions of the voice, of the incomparable lieder of Schubert, Schumann and Brahms, at his mother's side. His reputation as the leading music pedagogue of our day is richly deserved.

My lessons with Karl Ulrich, albeit often tests of endurance, were not without their less serious moments. On one occasion, finding myself unprepared for a lesson on a problematic Brahms Intermezzo, which was scheduled to take place that evening, I decided not to go to my office that day but to spend the entire time at home catching up on my many missed hours of practice. I had failed, however, to anticipate the fact that my back muscles simply could not stand the unaccustomed strain. By 8:00 P.M., I was in anguish and flung myself on a couch next to the piano, praying that some miracle would delay Schnabel's imminent arrival.

But the doorbell rang, announcing his arrival at the appointed time. Entering the room, he stood with all his commanding six foot stature and looked down on me as I lay supinely on the couch. Omitting all amenities, I looked up at him and pronounced with finality: "If I could, I would throw this Steinway out of that window!"

His reply was crisp: "How fortunate that you don't play the flute," and, turning to the piano, he proclaimed imperiously, "You are here! I am here! Brahms is there! Let us begin." Caught in the magic of the Brahms score, abetted by Schnabel's inspirational teaching, my backache soon became a distant memory, reaffirming unmistakably the healing powers of music.

Some years later I had the privilege of introducing the first of Karl Schnabel's Master Classes at the Mannes School of Music in New York, where I served on the Board of Directors.

Some of today's leading pianists, such as Peter Serkin and Richard Goode, have been the beneficiaries of Schnabel's unique eighty-seven master classes, which have over the years developed many future concert artists both here and abroad.

Music Lesson in London

In 1946, Fiorello La Guardia, then Director General of the United Nations Relief and Rehabilitation Administration (UNRRA), sent me to represent the United States on a mission to Europe and the Middle East.

The purpose of the mission was to secure from certain governments the promised allotments of food to be distributed to the starving, homeless refugees of the war.

The representatives of the mission were to meet first in London, where at the UNRRA headquarters we would prepare a program and set quotas for the contributing countries before departing for Cairo, our first stop.

Among the many broken appointments I had to leave behind me in New York was a session with the elder Schnabel. This was to be one of those rugged music exchanges that had always terrified me. Like a schoolboy with a note excusing him from school, I phoned Schnabel and announced that I would have to cancel the lesson.

Obviously unimpressed, Schnabel asked, "When will you be in London?"

"Next Thursday," I told him, "for a few days." "Fine," he shot back, "I'll be there at the same time for a concert with the London Philharmonic. You will take your lesson at my studio in the Hyde Park Hotel, on Friday at five o'clock." He hung up. His tone had left no room for objection. To a Schnabel, a trip across the Atlantic was no excuse for missing a music session.

On that Friday, I was deeply immersed in the second full-day meeting with my associates, the representatives from Canada, France and England. We were gathering together statistical proof to support our contention that both the Turkish and Egyptian governments had the financial ability to make good their promised but sorely delinquent contributions to UNRRA.

At 4:00 P.M., I calmly announced to the chairman of the meeting that I had to leave. Even now I have to smile when I recall the expressions on the faces of my colleagues when, in answer to the chairman's question as to the reason for my leaving, I replied, "I have to take a music lesson."

To dispel their looks of dismay and disbelief, I added the details, mentioning that my teacher was Artur Schnabel. This almost broke up the meeting, for the concert was to be his first appearance in London since before the war. He was to play three Beethoven concertos and tickets were scarce; in fact, they were impossible to buy at any price.

Characteristically, it was the secretary who had the temerity to ask the question on the minds of everyone in the room. She asked me if I could appeal to my "friend in court" to get them tickets for the concert. With no great enthusiasm, I promised to try.

Promptly at 5:00 P.M., I made my appearance in Schnabel's suite. The Bechstein grand was there almost staring at me like a threatening monster. But once the amenities were over and we were immersed in the music, it was sheer inspiration.

Before leaving, I casually mentioned the meeting I had left and discreetly inquired about the possibility of getting tickets for my colleagues.

"By all means," was Schnabel's typically positive and forthright reply, "they are all invited to be my guests in my box. And I would be honored to have them come to the reception Sir Robert Mayer is giving after the concert."

It was a great evening which everyone enjoyed, no one more than Schnabel. And on this harmonious note, the mission flew off to the Middle East.

Practicing Ten Minutes Every Day

Shortly before Schnabel left for his summer retreat in his beloved Swiss mountains, I met with him to bid him au revoir. It was 1951 and his illness and loss of eyesight gave me forebodings that this might be our last meeting. As we parted, he reached for my hand.

"Promise me," he said, "that you will practice for ten minutes every day."

It seemed such a minor and surprising request that I naturally assented. How touching that the great man had my interest enough at heart to concern himself about my piano studies. It was a form of painless persuasion that he was employing to keep me from abandoning my work at the piano in the light of the many activities that called upon my time.

But as every piano student knows, it is impossible to practice for precisely ten minutes; it could be nine minutes, or twelve or twenty minutes. What the promise really meant was that an appointment with the piano each day would constitute my commitment to continuous music-making. Since then, the habit of daily practice has become so ingrained in me that a day that begins without a warm-up at the instrument is a day built on a void.

It soon became evident that the routine of "practicing for ten minutes every day" ran head-on into my extensive schedule of travel throughout the country to fulfill my many business and lecture engagements. To make certain there would be a piano available for me at each hotel at which I stayed, I devised a form letter which was mailed to the manager of each hotel in advance of my arrival. It requested the manager to arrange to have a piano available for my use during my stay at his hotel, regardless of the type of instrument or its location; even an aged upright in a remote corner would serve my purpose.

This request, which I must say was respected in almost every instance, resulted in some bizarre episodes. One memorable one occurred in Jerusalem in 1961. I had gone to Israel as correspondent of *Look* magazine, and I was also to testify at the trial of Adolf Eichmann, the infamous Nazi who led the mass murders of Jews.

The manager of the King David Hotel at which I stayed in Jerusalem turned out to be a Rumanian Jew who remembered that I had been instrumental in saving his life in 1944 and put every kind of hospitality at my disposal.

One afternoon, after testifying at the Eichmann trial, just as I returned to my hotel room, my telephone rang and the operator informed me that there was a group of reporters in the lobby waiting to interview me. But their timing conflicted with my scheduled appointment with the small grand piano located in a rear room on the first floor of the hotel. I grabbed my precious score of a Schubert Impromptu, but when the door of the elevator opened on the first floor, I found myself surrounded by reporters. They immediately began to pepper me with questions regarding my testimony at the trial dealing with Joel Brand, the Hungarian Jew who had been sent by Eichmann on a nefarious mission to exchange Jewish lives for trucks and money during the closing weeks of World War II.

To the dismay of the reporters, I put them off by announcing quietly, "I can't talk to you now, I have to practice the piano, but it will only take ten minutes." I moved off towards the rear of the hotel with the astonished reporters in pursuit. To fend them off, I gave them permission to attend the practice session, and they agreed to wait.

Next morning a story in the *London Times* datelined "Jerusalem" carried the headline: "Schubert Takes Precedence Over Eichmann."

Another episode resulting from my promise to Schnabel that I would practice the piano for "ten minutes every day" occurred in San Francisco. As consultant to a Canadian client, I was investigating the purchase of a major piece of real estate in the area and sought the advice of my friend Ben Swig, who owned the Fairmont Hotel at which I was staying. I also took advantage of my visit to San Francisco to arrange for a piano lesson on the challenging Mozart Rondo in A which I had been studying with Karl Schnabel prior to his having gone to that city to teach.

At the end of my conversation with Ben Swig about the real estate deal, I asked him if he would help me locate a piano in his large hostelry. Astonished by this unexpected change of subject, he asked as though he could hardly believe his ears, "What for?" I must confess, my offbeat request did sound a bit incongruous after the million-dollar real estate deal we had been discussing.

"I have a piano lesson in an hour," I told him blandly, "and I have to practice."

"You have to do what?" he almost shouted, cocking his head as though he thought he might not have heard me correctly. But when I continued to insist that I needed a piano because I had a lesson scheduled in an hour and had to practice, he shook his head resignedly and sent for his hotel's manager who directed me to a large banquet hall in the basement where I found a grand piano. A group of waiters were at the moment utilizing the piano's top as a receptacle on which they were unfolding the large white damask tablecloths they were to put on the tables for the banquet to take place there that evening.

I went over to the piano chair but found it much too low. I asked the bedazzled waiters if they would help me find something I could place on the chair to raise my sitting position.

"No problem at all," was their ready response. Immediately several of them reached for the pile of white tablecloths, and folding them to the size of a cushion, they plumped them down on the piano stool and motioned for me to sit down on them. I did so, and finding myself now properly elevated, I began my practice session. The waiters asked for permission to listen. When I agreed, because they were apparently delighted by the pleasant diversion, they abandoned their work and gathered eagerly around the piano.

I can't recall how the session went, but it must have impressed the waiters and excited their admiration, for when I was finished and asked them what they planned to do with the tablecloths on which I had sat, they replied that only very special guests would have the privilege of dining on the tablecloths which had supported my posterior.

Clearly, in spite of the hotel owner's dubious concern, my practice session had served to provide the waiters with a pleasant interlude and a respite from their routine labors. The impromptu service of the piano and the tablecloths had apparently also served me well, as it is my recollection that the music lesson later that day with Karl Schnabel was exceptionally successful.

Schnabel's Last Concert

In 1951, with typical insouciance and positiveness, Artur Schnabel revealed that a deep personal tragedy had befallen him. A few days before he was to give a concert at Hunter College in New York, he phoned me and announced almost exultantly that he had made an astonishing discovery: he could play the piano without looking at the keys. I understood immediately that this was his way of reporting that his failing eyesight was worsening rapidly as the cataracts descended upon him.

I tried to minimize my sorrow and concern by mentioning my lessons with his son and the Beethoven Sonata Opus 90 which I was then studying. "Good," he replied, "I think I'll include it in my program."

His performance at the concert, which proved to be his last appearance in America, did not reveal any sign his eyesight was failing but rose to new spiritual heights. Karl and I sat together listening with heavy hearts, for we sensed that he was approaching a grand finale in his career.

I phoned Schnabel the next morning to thank him for the joy he had once again provided with his memorable Beethoven, and prudently put a question to him about the Opus 90 Sonata. I had noticed a distinct difference and change in his interpretation since he had recorded the piece, especially in the accelerando which ends it.

"Of course," he said with characteristic ebullience, "I hope I improve every day."

In those few words he had revealed, with simple humility, the secret of his ever-affirmative formula of forward movement in his art and in his life. Even with failing eyesight and the heart ailment that would end his life two months later, the standards and the perseverance, which had been the hallmarks of the life and career of this giant personality, had not for a single moment abandoned him.

I was at my home in Water Mill, Long Island, when the news of Schnabel's death in Switzerland reached me on August 15, 1951.

My immediate impulse was to walk alone toward the ocean to ponder the impact of my loss. A luminous star in my universe had suddenly dimmed. As I made my way toward the rolling surf, captured by the majesty and rhythm, I felt myself breathing the sublime rhythm of Schubert's Impromptu from Opus 90, as Schnabel had played it in his last performance in New York, and was able to take strength from the bottomless reservoir of musical understanding that my great friend had left with me.

That evening I arranged a memorial concert program on my FM radio station WABF, which was dedicated to good classical music. Three of Franz Schubert's piano sonatas were played on recordings into which Schnabel had breathed eternal life. I quote here excerpts from the tribute which I paid to my immortal friend on that program.

> The passing of Artur Schnabel leaves a void in our musical and civilized life which cannot be filled. Few people have been fortunate enough to know the consummateness of his art and to realize how vital a part Schnabel played in elevating and maintaining the standards of programs and performances.
>
> In a way he was a kind of musical 'conscience' for conductors and other musicians. He put art above the person and conducted a one-man war against the Philistines of our time. This applied not only to music, which was his medium, but also to politics, as when he spoke out against Hitler and Fascism.
>
> Never in the several decades during which I knew him and worked with him can I recall a single instance where he made a concession to commercialism or compromised his conception of the music for convenience.
>
> "Music is better than musicians," and "Beethoven is better than the people who play him," are among the telling aphorisms he so enjoyed making.
>
> In the fields of music and philosophy Schnabel exerted an enormous influence over me and over anyone who was exposed to the fire of his intense zeal for the higher life—and to his abiding wisdom. Some years ago, I had occasion to bring Schnabel together with Supreme Court Justice Felix Frankfurter.
>
> 'No other man I've met, excepting Justice Holmes, has so much wisdom to give,' Justice Frankfurter confided to me after having a two-hour discussion with Schnabel.
>
> To all of us, his legion of friends and pupils in all parts of the world, he gave something through his spirit and his music which will remain with us throughout our lives.

Chapter Five

Fighting Furtwängler Perfidy

Blockade of Philharmonic Post

The dismal prophecy of the destruction of the Jews that I had heard uttered by Hitler in his own raucous voice in 1932 was by 1936 becoming a harsh reality. As the Nazis' anti-Semitic juggernaut gained momentum, it reached into the Berlin Symphony Orchestra, where the conductor, Wilhelm Furtwängler, dismissed all Jewish players.

Ignoring Furtwängler's record of compliance with Hitler's anti-Semitic dictates, the Board of Directors of the New York Philharmonic voted to engage him to replace the world's most celebrated conductor and the public's idol, Arturo Toscanini.

The news of Furtwängler's engagement, following the announcement of Toscanini's imminent departure, reverberated as a second shock for American music lovers.

The two conductors represented diametrically opposing political philosophies. Toscanini, the fiery lover of freedom, had cut short his career in Italy by refusing to join the legions of Mussolini, the "Sawdust Caesar." Only a few months earlier, the Maestro had led a group of eleven internationally known artists in resigning from the Wagner Festival in Bayreuth, Germany, in protest against the persecution of Jews and others in Germany.

Furtwängler, on the other hand, had bowed and scraped before Hitler and his Nazi stooges, acquiesced to their anti-Semitic demands, and had accepted many honors from them.

The engagement of Furtwängler by the New York Philharmonic embroiled me in one of the most critical battles of my public life. It seemed not only an affront to the American public in general, but a demonstration of callous disregard for the feelings of others to bring Furtwängler to New York, the city with the world's largest Jewish community. I felt this action demanded an immediate and forceful protest, so I called Felix Warburg, the banker, art patron and member of the Philharmonic Board who had been designated to extend the invitation to Furtwängler. I expressed my objections to Mr. Warburg, both as an American opposed to Fascism and as a fellow Jew. For my pains I was told, politely of course, that the Board had made its decision and it was too late to rescind it.

I found myself fighting upstream, virtually alone. I tried to form a protest committee, but only those few ineffectual "regulars" who support all liberal causes joined. None of the leading figures in the music world would respond. I soon learned that most of the so-called "art-patrons" were mainly motivated by the desire to improve their social status. In fact, they clearly resented my disturbing their secure and well-ordered lives by introducing an unpleasant political issue into the music world.

When I attempted to reach various members of the Philharmonic Board in order to present my point of view, only one, Minnie Guggenheim, was even willing to listen. She invited me to dinner with Edward L. Bernays, the public relations expert, but all they did was try to dissuade me from my course.

I sent the members of the Board a barrage of telegrams which were ignored. But copies of the wires were sent to the newspapers, and the story was given front page coverage. William Henderson of *The New York Sun*, dean of New York's music critics, devoted a full column to the "elephant-hide insensitivity of the Philharmonic Board."

The Philharmonic concert which followed the announcement of

Furtwängler's engagement was to be one of Toscanini's valedictory performances. In spite of warnings that I would suffer snubs and insults, I resolved to attend, as my two empty aisle seats could be interpreted as avoiding "facing the music" of the seething political issue.

I was surprised and pleased when my attractive friend Dorothy Schiff, a niece of Felix Warburg, called and asked if she could sit with me at the concert. It was her way of standing beside me publicly, and I gratefully escorted her as my guest. There were gasps of astonishment, especially from Dorothy's friends, when we arrived at Carnegie Hall and as we walked down the aisle to my seats.

Outside the hall a group of pretty young women was marching back and forth carrying signs which read: "Vote against Furtwängler and Hitler." Another group of women was distributing ballots on which were places one could mark a vote for either "Hitler and Furtwängler" or "Toscanini and Music." Admittedly, this demonstration was not entirely spontaneous, for I had garnered the attractive protesters from the social-register Junior League Club.

As predicted, during the intermission I was snubbed by people with whom I had chatted amiably each Thursday evening in the lobby of Carnegie Hall. Aside from one or two curt remarks about my having stirred up "this mess," no one spoke to me. It was a one-man fight and the odds were against me, but I was resolved to carry it on.

I was briefly heartened when one Saturday afternoon my secretary at Saks Fifth Avenue announced that two members of the Philharmonic Board were waiting to see me. I hoped they had come to join me and that their visit signaled a breach in the solid line drawn up against me, but this was not the case. They had come only to advise me in a paternal way that it would be best for me if I changed my course. While they were in my office, my telephone rang; on the other end was Mayor Fiorello La Guardia, whose unmistakable falsetto filled the room.

There was an elevator operators strike going on in New York at the time, and the Mayor had just succeeded in bringing representatives of the employers' group and the Union together in his office.

"I've locked those fellows in a room and I won't let them out until they come to an agreement," the Mayor squeaked with evident enjoyment. He added that while they were talking he planned to sneak out to the Metropolitan Opera to hear *Fidelio* and wanted me to come along.

Holding the phone slightly away from my ear to make sure that my visitors could hear the Mayor, I answered in a full voice, "I'm sorry, Fiorello, I'd like to join you, you know *Fidelio* is my favorite opera, but I have to stay and finish off this Furtwängler fight now that I have them on the run."

"The hell with them," the Mayor exploded, "I'll help you finish them. The music will be a shot in the arm for you, so meet me at two in the Bliss box. But remember, we'll have to sit in the back so we won't be seen." I assented, which brought a chuckle from Fiorello with the closing comment, "While we're listening to music, those fellows in my office will have to listen to each other."

At the opera we sat like truants in the back of the box and relished Beethoven's heroic score. The Mayor had been right, *Fidelio* did give me strength.

But Judson and his acquiescent Board were not on the run and displayed no intention of capitulating. Instead, they now brought to bear their heaviest weapon: financial pressure. Some of the members of the Philharmonic Board were also directors of Gimbel Brothers, which controlled Saks Fifth Avenue. They urged the Chairman, Bernard Gimbel, to silence me on the grounds that my activities could make enemies for the store. Mr. Gimbel brought the matter to my attention in what I admit was not an unkind manner, but I could not back down. I could only promise I would try to do my best to keep my name and that of the store out of the newspapers. But the pressure was beginning to tell on me. The cost in time and energy as well as in money was beginning to pile up at an alarming rate. I was not far from defeat.

Then, suddenly, the miracle we always hoped for happened. A young woman, I should say an angel, came to my rescue. One day, Nora Shea,

Arthur Judson's secretary, phoned me and insisted that I meet her secretly for lunch as she had important information for me.

We met in one of those tea rooms which are one flight up from the street. She was amazingly unfazed by the enormity of her violation of office internal security. Speaking softly she said, "Ira, I was afraid you might be cracking up! I just had to speak to you because what they are doing to you at the office is shameful." Leaning across the table and speaking almost in a whisper, she added, "You must hold out, it will only take a few more days. The office is being deluged by cancellations of subscriptions. At this rate very soon they will have no audience and no money. They just cannot go on."

I was overcome. This was my first indication that I was not alone and that my protest had not gone unheard. I will never forget her encouraging intercession. Why had she risked her job to help me? Perhaps it was a case of "bread cast upon the waters . . . " for my only previous personal contact with my "angel" had been during a voyage to Europe. Knowing we were both to be on board the same ocean liner, Bruno Zirato, Assistant Manager of the Philharmonic, had asked me to introduce her to some people during the trip, and I had done so. In addition I had invited her to join me and my friends at several parties which had apparently enhanced and shortened her first voyage across the Atlantic.

Two days after my rendezvous with her, I was overjoyed to receive a gracefully stated, almost fulsome invitation from Felix Warburg to visit him at his Fifth Avenue home. I took special delight in accepting. It ended with my helping to draft a cable in Furtwängler's name to the Board of the Philharmonic. The next night, pedestrians on Times Square must have wondered at the young man who stood bareheaded and enthralled watching the moving letters of the great electric sign that encircled the Times Building as they spelled out a headline from the next morning's edition of *The New York Times*:

FURTWÄNGLER DECLINES APPOINTMENT AS MUSIC
DIRECTOR OF PHILHARMONIC DUE TO ILLNESS.

The passers-by could not have known that to me these were not just letters on a moving electric belt; for me the words were set to music—almost a personal paean of triumph.

Proof of Collusion

The rejection of Furtwängler, so soon after the news of Toscanini's "departure," sent a tremor through the music world. I was the target of criticism from a number of musicians; not the least among them was the violinist Yehudi Menuhin, who publicly defended his "friend" Furtwängler. I was accused of having deprived American music audiences of performances by one of the world's leading conductors, whereas I had merely been trying to keep a renegade of music at a safe distance from our shores in a period of darkest threat to the culture of our society. Even today, nearly a half century later, misinterpretations of my motives are still occasionally heard; the repercussions of that battle have never quite died down.

Furtwängler claimed that he had had no choice, that he had been forced to bow to Hitler's demands and fire the Jewish players in his orchestra to save himself. But this is too narrow a personal escape hatch for him to crawl through in the light of the actions of so many of his distinguished colleagues. If they could choose voluntary exile rather than submit to Nazi dictates, Furtwängler's abject surrender to the Fascist leaders cannot be condoned.

In view of the controversy concerning Furtwängler's conduct during the Hitler years, when in Berlin on a U.S. government mission immediately after the war, I pursued the matter and discovered in United States Army archives a document containing the following excerpt:

> ... it shamefully fails to mention that the hero of 1934 (Furtwängler) had made his peace with the Nazis; that he made a statement of loyalty in which he expressly approved of Adolf Hitler's cultural politics and recognized National Socialism as the best form of government for Germany's welfare; that the title of State Counselor was bestowed upon him, as well as the yearly stipend of (10,000 Reichsmarks) which went

along with it; that for the Proclamation of the Jewish Laws at the Nuremberg Party Rally he directed Beethoven; and that again and again he allowed himself to be sent abroad as the cultural emissary of the Third Reich. If he had followed the advice which so many people offered him and left the Third Reich as Toscanini did, perhaps today he would be a candidate for the presidency of a free Germany.

A deep moral and ethical issue is involved here, in which there is no room for compromise. There is no halfway measure by which a leading, world-celebrated figure can align himself with the enemy, especially when the issue of freedom is at stake. One who makes a deal with the enemy must pay a price. The payment that Furtwangler was obliged to make, as I viewed it in those critical days when the forces of freedom were struggling against Fascism, was that he be denied the privilege of using his prestige as a leading music-maker to escape his moral responsibility as a man. He could not be permitted to serve the Nazis in a major post and at the same time become Music Director of the free world's most important symphony orchestra. For an acknowledged accomplice of Adolf Hitler to stand on both the podium of the Berlin Symphony Orchestra and on that of the New York Philharmonic in Carnegie Hall would be an unparalleled example of political acrobatics.

To those who continue to maintain that art and politics must be kept separate and apart, my answer is: Men who have become celebrated figures in the art world and accept the admiration of the public must remember that the accolades imply an obligation to maintain a quality of moral leadership in all their actions.

Bronislaw Hubermann's reply to Furtwängler's request that he continue to work in Berlin expressed a spirit of repugnance at the effort of a state to control art and artists more poignantly and with deeper effect than in any other published document when he said:

> In reality it is not a question of violin concertos, or even merely of the Jews; the issue is the retention of those things achieved by our fathers through blood and sacrifice; the elementary pre-conditions of our culture; the freedom of personality and its unconditional self-responsibility unhampered by fetters of caste or race.

In Nazi Germany, a commission of four, one of them Furtwängler, was set up to be the central control over all music in Germany. The steps by which the State took over musical life in that country, and the elimination of all individuals not sympathetic to the politics and proscriptions of the Nazi government, followed.

In April 1933, Fritz Busch, not a Jew, was forcibly removed from his post as musical director of the Dresden Opera. The Minister of Culture in Berlin canceled a scheduled series of Brahms chamber music by the eminent musicians Artur Schnabel, Bronislaw Hubermann, Gregor Piatigorsky and Paul Hindemith. Adolf Busch withdrew from the Hamburg Brahms centennial in protest after his son-in-law and protégé, the pianist Rudolf Serkin, had been denied permission to participate in the celebration.

Schnabel decided to leave Germany following the cancellation of his participation in the Brahms festival because he was Jewish. Furtwängler begged Schnabel to play again with him in Germany. "Not until every Jewish artist and every Jewish orchestra player is welcome in Germany," was Schnabel's reply.

The most significant event connected with German music that took place during Hitler's regime was Toscanini's refusal to conduct at the Bayreuth Festival. On April 1, 1933, Toscanini sent Hitler a cable stating he was withdrawing from the Festival as a protest against the persecution of his colleagues in Germany. Hitler never acknowledged the cable, but on April 4, the German government issued an edict banning the broadcasting of any music performed or composed by any of the eleven famous musicians who had also signed the cable.

In June, Toscanini sent a message to Frau Winifried Wagner, stating his reasons for withdrawing from the Bayreuth Wagner Festival in these words:

> The lamentable events which have wounded my feelings both as man and as artist have not to this moment changed, despite my hopes. It is my duty today to break the silence I have imposed on myself for the last two months, and to inform you that for my, your and everybody else's tranquility, it is better not to think anymore of my going to Bayreuth.

With unchanged sentiments of affectionate friendship towards the
entire Wagner family, I am yours,

Arturo Toscanini

This cancellation caused an international sensation and was a terrible
blow to the Hitler government, for Toscanini was to have been the star attraction at Bayreuth.

After the war, Furtwängler made the following statement in his own
defense:

> What kept me in Germany was my anxiety to preserve German music in
> its integrity. I could not do that from abroad. When Thomas Mann asks,
> How can Beethoven be played in Himmler's Germany? I reply, Where
> was the music of Beethoven more needed than in Hitler's Germany?
> I could not, therefore, quit Germany in her hour of greatest need.

Nothing that Furtwängler could have said for the record could possibly
have condemned him with more finality than his own words, which confirmed
his outright collusion with Fascism. Perhaps his confusion can be ascribed to
his inability to distinguish between morality and self-interest, but a man who
is able to embrace, memorize and perform the universal works of Beethoven
from the podium as he did so superbly, cannot be accused of stupidity. If nothing else, it demonstrates an abysmal lack of judgment and of moral character.

By acknowledging Thomas Mann's description of the Germany at that
time as "Himmler's Germany," he casts an insulting aspersion on the nature
of true pre-Nazi German culture. Furtwängler, of all people, should have understood that the real German culture could never remotely belong to Himmler
or to any individual, for it is a treasure belonging to all mankind. His claim of
keeping German culture alive is preposterous under a Fascist regime guilty
of the degradation of culture and of genocide on a scale unparalleled in history.

Furtwängler's defenders must be reminded that the Germany of Beethoven
and Bach belongs to the universe, and that it survived without protection by
any single musician. The gangsters with whom Furtwängler collaborated
are remembered for their onslaught on all civilization, for their burning of
books and for the conflagrations they ignited in a Holocaust against their

own innocent people. That Furtwängler felt a personal need to separate himself from his illustrious colleagues who had the courage and integrity to abandon their homeland when its artistic life was being desecrated by Hitler, speaks volumes in itself.

Furtwängler's own words are transparent opportunism and reveal his cowardice. In choosing to associate himself with the Third Reich, he chose the enemy of all art and culture. Fortunately, German culture stands securely on the roots of Thomas Mann, Beethoven, Goethe, and the many other deathless exponents of the deep legacy of Germany art.

It is hoped that this corrected and updated chronicle of the sordid record of the brilliant musician's behavior in the face of the Fascist challenge to the world, will say *"finis"* to the controversy which has too long surrounded the "Affaire Furtwängler": that it will once and for all bury this sordid episode among the achives of the Hitler nightmare.

Chapter Six

Two Geniuses of the Podium

The Revival of Otto Klemperer

The New York Philharmonic Orchestra's schedule of four concerts a week at Carnegie Hall along with daily rehearsals was too grueling a task for any one conductor to maintain for a full season of twenty-eight weeks. In 1936, the first half of the season was conducted by Arturo Toscanini. For the second half the highly touted German Otto Klemperer was engaged.

The contrast in personality on the stage between Klemperer and the Italian Maestro could not have been more pronounced. Each was a taskmaster who achieved superlative results from the orchestra with his own individual style and technique. Because of his towering height, six-feet six inches, Klemperer conducted from the floor of the stage, dispensing with the podium used by all other conductors.

Yet Klemperer's stature was not to be measured in the physical but in the reach of his music and its soul. He beat time with spare, unobtrusive movements, using a slender six-inch stick, bending over at times and using his full arms to impose an almost granite-like rhythm on the orchestra. Toscanini, the graceful, courtly Italian, whipped a large baton which at times seemed a fiery extension of him, through the air in a magnetic circular motion that held his players and audiences in his grip. It was inevitable that any conductor who followed Toscanini did so at his own peril. Long after he had left his podium, the electric Toscanini personality and the inimitable color of his orchestra's sonority still seemed to hover over Carnegie Hall like an iridescent cloud.

It was not long before the contrasting personalities of the two conductors also became evident to the ladies of the Philharmonic Board, who vied with one another to use the conductors as drawing cards for their social teas. On the rare occasions when the Maestro permitted himself to be the social lion at a reception, his gracious, enchanting manner never failed to conquer the ladies.

As soon as Klemperer arrived on the scene he was invited to be the star attraction at an afternoon tea. Klemperer, who detested these nonmusical "command performances," begged me to accompany him in the hope that my presence might serve to ease his tension.

True to form, not long after our arrival, a plate of hors d'oeuvres and a cup of tea slipped from Klemperer's lap, spilling their contents on the floor with a resounding crash. From my seat at the opposite end of the room, I could almost feel the anguish of the giant figure positioned awkwardly between chattering ladies while a maid in uniform swept bits of food and china from the elegant rug. Klemperer signaled to me for help in making an early exit. We adjourned to a nearby Childs Restaurant.

Needless to say, the ladies' interest in further social functions with Klemperer evaporated. Since he had cultivated few American friends and kept them at arm's length, attendance in his reception room after each performance gradually diminished until it was reduced to just one person— me. Klemperer faced this social ostracism philosophically. He refused to permit extraneous activities to interfere with his demonic concentration on music-making. The Childs Restaurant on Eighth Avenue and Fifty-seventh Street became our Thursday night, post-concert refuge, where we would sit, drink tea and exchange views about music.

One of the most bizarre episodes which occurred while Klemperer was at the Philharmonic involved Bruno Labate, the orchestra's peerless oboist. At one evening's concert, Labate, who bore a striking resemblance to Fiorello La Guardia, even to his mobile facial expressions, did the unforgivable. In a symphony where the oboe takes over the theme on a note of rapture in the last movement, Labate's usually mellow and reliable instrument somehow managed to emit a sound not dissimilar to a sheep's bleat, completely destroying the dramatic climax Klemperer had built up. In a fury, the irate conductor shook his fist at Labate, calling out, "PIG!" in a voice loud enough to be heard by those seated in the first few rows of the hall.

As I made my way to the conductor's dressing room after the concert, I could hear Klemperer's booming voice. He was in a rage.

"How could he *do* it?" Klemperer roared. "He ruined the concert . . . where *is* he?"

But the pint-sized Labate knew his man and had been quick to beat a retreat with the other members of the orchestra into their dressing room. I had just succeeded in pacifying Klemperer as he was dressing, when I noticed the door of the room slowly opening. Out of a narrow crack the unmistakable head of Labate appeared. In a dulcet voice he uttered: "Maestro, I forgive you." The door slammed shut quickly. Klemperer's reaction was almost apoplectic. "*You* forgive *me*!" he roared, throwing his massive body toward the door, but Labate had vanished like quicksilver.

The story of the escapade was greatly enjoyed by the other musicians, who silently applauded their comrade's bravado and offered prayerful thanks that they had avoided the eye of the conductor's storm.

I learned that Mayor La Guardia had been in the audience that night, and when I described the defiance and escape of the plucky oboist, he was greatly amused. Some years later, my recall of the Labate episode would come to my rescue.

When La Guardia became Director General of UNRRA, he appointed me his personal representative, and I agreed to undertake a mission which included an inspection of all the refugee camps in post-war Europe. These DP (Displaced Persons) camps under the supervision of former British Brigadier Generals sent from London were in a deplorable condition. I lost no time in firing the Brigadiers as I could not find an excuse for their palpably negligent administration of the camps, which contained the emaciated starving remnant of European Jewry.

Toward the end of my tour of the camps, which covered most of Germany, I contracted pneumonia from my day-and-night exertions in cold, unheated buildings, and was obliged to return to London, where I found a cable from La Guardia awaiting me. Its implied criticism of my firing the Brigadiers had emanated from the British Foreign Office's complaint relayed to La Guardia by Secretary of State James F. Byrnes. While I had sought no acknowledgment or reward for my exhausting efforts, the unwarranted, stinging criticism in my feverish condition could not have come at a worse time. A meager dinner in my hotel in war-torn London added to my dispirited mood. After I had composed and discarded half a dozen sharp replies, suddenly, out of nowhere, the shrill discordant sound of Labate's oboe echoed in my memory. I immediately dispatched a cable to La Guardia which read:

"IN THE IMMORTAL WORDS OF LABATE, I FORGIVE YOU."

But the Labate episode was not the only discordant note in the descending scale of Klemperer's conductorship. As the Philharmonic's 1936 season progressed, Klemperer's audiences gradually diminished. The balance and purity of sound that he was able to extract from the orchestra were not enough to overcome his impersonal style and capture an audience still under the spell of the magnetic Toscanini. Facing rejection, Klemperer pleaded with Arthur Judson to grant him one final hour of redemption by permitting him to end his season with a performance of the sublime Ninth Symphony of Beethoven. To Judson, increasing the orchestra's deficit by incurring the extra expense of the chorus and soloists for the monumental Ninth Symphony was adding insult to injury, so he adamantly refused. Klemperer, in desper-

ation, turned to me and his friend Alexander Smallens, the conductor, pleading with us to intercede with Judson, who agreed to meet with us and
Klemperer at a luncheon at the Hotel Plaza.

In response to our urgent pleas and in order to dispose of the matter,
Judson reluctantly consented to the performance of the grand Beethoven
symphony. Before we could thank him, however, Klemperer intervened.
In his strong bass voice he announced: "All right. I will conduct the Mahler
Second Symphony." We could almost understand and sympathize with
Judson's frustration when he countered by saying, "You see what I have to
put up with?"

The performance of the Mahler Second Symphony in C turned out to be
an unqualified sensation. Klemperer sent to Budapest for contralto Enid
Szanto, whose voice had the perfect timbre for the music and lifted Mahler's
final incandescent pages to the heavens. The last movement took the house
by storm, and the critics were lyrical in their praise. At the repeat concerts
on Friday and Sunday afternoons, tickets were at a premium.

Klemperer's career, however, was to receive an abrupt jolt. He suffered
a stroke which paralyzed his right side, including his trusty right arm. The
tragedy of his collapse was compounded by the evaporation of all his friends,
with the exception of the composer Mark Brunswick and myself.

After Klemperer had spent several months in a Boston Hospital, he dis-
appeared. I finally located him recuperating alone in a shabby room on the
West Side in New York. He was immobilized in bed, totally dejected, convinced that he would never conduct again. To lift his spirits I suggested
that he could still conduct with his left arm, and to prove it, I offered him an
engagement to conduct a concert of my New Friends Orchestra at Town
Hall. As though grasping at a last straw, he agreed.

For the musicians of my little orchestra, the drama of his comeback
made their first rehearsal with him a never-to-be-forgotten experience.
He limped into the small hall, was helped to his feet, and faced the tense
group of young musicians. Suddenly he raised his left arm which came

down like a scimitar, and in his resounding bass voice called out in German: *"Also, eins!"* (Now, one!)

The response was electric. Lotte Hammerschlag, the ace string player who led the viola section of the orchestra, vividly remembers how the conductor's magic permeated the atmosphere as the Bach Brandenburg Concerto No. 6 sprang to life. It was as though the music, which had been pent up in him so long, had broken loose and was surging in a passionate torrent.

The concert at Town Hall was memorable both in terms of the re-creation of music and of the revival of the man's great powers. He gradually rebuilt his career, and at the time of his death in 1976 he was universally conceded to be one of the world's pre-eminent conductors.

Klemperer had originally come to America for a brief guest conductorship at the invitation of Walter Damrosch, Director of the New York Symphony Orchestra, which later merged with the Philharmonic. I had met Klemperer in the 1930s through Artur Schnabel and had been immediately attracted by the wholesome, unadorned dedication of his music-making. The unequaled purity, a distillation of sound from his orchestra together with his simple, self-effacing direction was a refreshing change from the virtuoso antics of many of his contemporaries.

From Wagner through Stravinsky, the musical institutions were financially supported by unmusical bankers, women with social ambition and less and less musical erudition. Rarely at a concert, other than chamber music, do the faces betray more than an exterior reaction and do you hear a discussion of the ideas behind the music. The applause, it seems to me, is a reaction to a release from a vacant, preoccupied distance.

A highly-geared technical performance will make them applaud—or even shout; but it never seems to lift them up and give happiness, which is music's goal. The effort of conductors for a driving effect or a luscious sound seems the limit of their musical conceptions, omitting the endless search for the inner voice in depth from the composer's meaning. The last performances of Otto Klemperer of Mozart symphonies are a lesson in luminosity.

Klemperer was the last of the giants of post-war Europe. There was a great contrast between his impersonalized performances and the forced virtuosity of Stokowski, the talent and superficiality of Mehta, and finally the overcharged high tension of Sir George Solti.

My contact with him was maintained with occasional letters, but mainly through his incomparable recordings. In 1971, while en route to Israel, I stopped off in London to see him and attended his tenth repeat performance of Beethoven's *Fidelio* at Covent Garden. Sitting with Klemperer's daughter, Lotte, in a box overlooking the orchestra, I watched as the giant Maestro was assisted like a wounded lion to a high chair facing the musicians and singers. Again, the imperious left hand rose and came down with its incisive beat to sound the inimitable chords of the challenging overture, which signals the opera's opening.

After the performance, Klemperer had arranged an informal reception for me with the cast of *Fidelio* at the Hyde Park Hotel. I treasure the memory of our quiet conversation at the party, which proved to be the last words we had together.

"How is it," I asked him, "that your orchestra is like a pool, one can hear every instrument separately, and yet they flow together as one?"

He leaned back, sucked at his pipe which Lotte had filled for him, turned to me and in an almost confiding tone said:

"You have always been one who can understand what it is that I try to make happen with music." His gaunt face and luminous eyes took on an expression of tenderness and affection born of a friendship that had been enriched by mutual experiences of music fulfillment and the vicissitudes which engulfed his life, many of which we had overcome together.

My Debt to Bruno Walter

One of the chronic problems opera composers have always faced is the paucity of suitable story material for librettos. Throughout his life, the immortal composer Giuseppi Verdi suffered desperately in his search for worthy story material. In his later years he fused his genius with Shakespeare, which resulted in the operatic masterpieces of *Macbeth*, *Otello* and *Falstaff* based on the Bard's epic dramas. Hector Berlioz, too, had turned to Shakespeare's *King Lear* and *Romeo and Juliet* for the story in two of his timeless creations.

Verdi's celebrated *La Forza del Destino* was a great favorite of mine, and the magnetic quality of its music drew me to the opera again and again. But the libretto supplied by F. Piave of Venice defied my repeated efforts to follow its story line, and I had abandoned all hope of cutting through its torturous threads.

In 1941, Bruno Walter's charming daughter, Lotte, invited me to a performance of the enigmatic *Forza* at the Metropolitan Opera to be conducted by her father.

Here was my chance to confront the distinguished conductor after the performance for clarification of the text. Having frequently conducted the opera he would certainly have an intimate knowledge of the meaning of its libretto. At the reception which followed the performance, I cornered the genial music director and put my question to him, adding a note of apology for my "ignorance." Imagine my shock when he replied, "Don't apologize, I too have been trying for years to make out the plot from the conductor's pit."

To have such distinguished company in my frustration did provide a measure of solace but was of no help in my efforts to unravel the thorny threads of the story, which to this day I have been unable to piece together. So I have resolved to settle down in my seat at the opera at performances of *Forza*, eyes closed, and let the music of the "force of destiny" take over completely through the overpowering score of Giuseppe Verdi. My conviction had been affirmed that the opera form is not truly a fusion of the arts; for the greatest story not matched with great music cannot make a successful opera, while great music matched with a weak plot can still result in an operatic masterpiece.

Bruno Walter was a man of exquisite sensitivity who breathed music. It was the qualities of gentility and persuasion that animated his direction, which won the respect and hearts of the somewhat "hardened" orchestra players of the Philharmonic, and drew from them the utmost responsiveness. This was achieved in contrast to Toscanini's personality, style, commanding presence, and uncompromising demands.

Walter's performance of the Beethoven G Major Piano Concerto No. 4, which opened the Philharmonic's 1933 season with the return of his colleague Artur Schnabel to this country, remains unforgettable due to the rare rapport achieved by the two great Beethoven interpreters at the height of their careers.

I owe Lotte Walter the description of how the two intimate friends enjoyed the weekly rite of a stroll around the reservoir in New York's Central Park. They would walk arm in arm, European style while, Lotte Walter reported rudely, "Father walked and Schnabel talked."

But Walter, by no means reticent but richly eloquent, enjoyed a unique brand of articulation of his own. His personality combined the qualities of the nineteenth century romantic with the spirituality of a mystic, and infused his supreme music-making with a compassion that imparted a feeling of comfort to his listeners.

"When he accompanies me," Lotte Lehmann once said, "I have a feeling of the utmost well-being and security. His baton is like a cradle in which he rocks me."

Walter believed that creators of great music are endowed with something close to divinity. Music was to him truly a religion, a spiritual emanation addressed to us from God. I was witness to his affinity for matching the glory of Bach's music to quotations from the Bible. During an evening in my home, following a discourse with Schnabel, he turned to the piano and translated his fervor with an impromptu reading of a passage from Ecclesiastes with the musical accompaniment from one of Bach's cantatas.

Chapter Seven

La Guardia and Music

Creating the High School of Music and Art

In 1933 I became a member of Fiorello La Guardia's "kitchen cabinet" when I joined his historic uphill campaign to replace the corrupt Tammany Hall gang which had driven New York city to the edge of bankruptcy. The former five-term Congressman had already become a colorful and nationally known figure from his dramatic personality, his legislative innovations and relentless fight against organized crime. My friendship with him began during his campaign but grew into real intimacy only after we discovered that we shared an addiction to good music.

At first I attended Thursday evening Philharmonic concerts with him at Carnegie Hall, where we sat in his seats in the top balcony (which he kept even after his election as Mayor of New York). Later we attended many concerts together; he and his wife Marie rarely missed any of my New Friends concerts in their aisle seats as guests at Town Hall.

La Guardia's love of music began in his early childhood. His father, Achille, was a musician who had come to the United States originally as accompanist to Adelina Patti, and remained to become a grandmaster. He taught Fiorello to play the cornet, and his daughter Gemma the piano. The two regularly played duets at social functions in their home town of Prescott, Arizona, where Fiorello spent his happy formative years.

La Guardia's interest in music grew and deepened with time, and even during the crowded years while he was Mayor of New York, he always managed to find time to attend concerts at Carnegie Hall and go to the Met.

When La Guardia was elected Mayor in November of 1934, it was with a sense of satisfaction that I considered my efforts in his successful campaign a closed chapter. To have played a part in his historic victory over the corrupt forces which had so long undermined the city was for me reward enough. But about a week after the election I received a letter from him asking almost petulantly where I had "been hiding." I replied that with the campaign over, I had nothing special to see him about. He then phoned me, and we made a date to meet at his office. When I arrived, I found myself surrounded by reporters. Calling me in, La Guardia turned to the reporters, pointed at me and said: "See this guy, he can have any job he wants in my administration." He went on to hint about Commissioner of Welfare. I was cornered. To refuse him point blank after his laudatory comments to the press, would have been an embarrassment to him. But I had no intention of entering public life, especially not under La Guardia. His friendship was a prized possession which I did not want to risk losing, as I realized that we were both extreme individualists with short-fused tempers which could ignite under too close an association. So I rejected his grandstand offer as gracefully as possible and made an exit. I did say as I was leaving that I was interested in education and would be glad to serve in that field as long as it was not a paying job.

Shortly after La Guardia took office as Mayor of New York I wrote him a letter in which I outlined an idea dealing with education that had been fermenting in my mind for a long time. From my own experience of being educated in the public schools in Baltimore I had observed the squandering of the talents of students gifted in the arts. They were obliged to study all the routine subjects but were provided with only the most minimal exposure to those areas for which they had special interest and ability. My suggestion to La Guardia was that New York City should establish a special high school which in addition to instruction in the required subjects would provide an enriched program of teaching music and art. The idea caught fire with the Mayor, and in a postscript to a letter on another subject he wrote, "Come down to City Hall so we can discuss your idea." He was quick to give my concept his blessing, which resulted in the creation of the High School of Music and Art in 1936. It was the nation's first high school in which gifted students could receive special training and comprehensive education in the fields of art and music. The new school became La Guardia's pet project. He called it "my baby" and sent it many gifts. Among them was a bust of Toscanini by his sculptor friend Onorio Ruotolo. He had it cast in bronze and placed on a pedestal where it dominated the entrance hall of the school. The historic growth of the school and its widening influence as a center for education in the arts was a hallmark of La Guardia's administration.

Over the years the High School of Music and Art developed into a hospitable haven where an increasing number of students were provided with the opportunity to concentrate in their chosen fields. Many of today's leading musicians, including Pinchas Zuckerman, the violinist; Catherine Malfitano, Metropolitan Opera star; Emanuel Ax, pianist; Stanley Drucker, clarinetist; James Conlin, conductor; and others owe their careers to the early training they received at New York's High School of Music and Art.

Dr. Benjamin Steigman was a fortunate choice as the school's first principal. His tireless dedication to the highest educational ideals throughout the twenty-two years of his stewardship was largely responsible for its broad development and excellence. In his valuable book, *Accent on Talent*, which covers the full history of the school, Dr. Steigman relates:

> La Guardia would often bring important musical organizations to the school, such as Ira Hirschmann's New Friends of Music and Thomas Sherman's Little Orchestra Society. They would hold rehearsals on the stage of the school's auditorium, with a microphone enabling students to hear and benefit from the professional conductor's instructions to his musicians.

These rehearsals came about through another suggestion which I made to La Guardia. After I had established the New Friends Orchestra, I recalled the "rehearsal-concerts" I had heard during my own high school days in Baltimore, by the Baltimore Symphony Orchestra, and offered to have the New Friends Orchestra hold its final rehearsal prior to a public performance at the school for the students. I invited La Guardia to attend the first of the New Friends Orchestra's "rehearsal concerts" at the school and to be the intermission speaker. It was a memorable morning. I can still recall the air of eagerness and excitement that swept through the crowded auditorium as the orchestra of young musicians played their hearts out for their youthful audience, which, along with La Guardia's zestful intermission talk, held the students spellbound.

The High School of Music and Art on Convent Avenue and 135th Street gradually outgrew the facilities of its original building. It was combined with the High School of the Performing Arts, a school established in 1948 to provide training for boys and girls who wished to prepare themselves for professional careers as dancers and actors. The two schools came together in 1961 in anticipation of their move near Lincoln Center, into a building designed to meet the specialized needs of the two unique areas of instruction. In 1969, the Board of Education honored Mayor La Guardia by naming the school after him. We owe the concept of combining the two schools and locating them near Lincoln Center to the noted composer William Schumann, former President of the Juilliard School and the first President of Lincoln Center. The combined school, which was opened in 1984, is directed by the energetic and resourceful Richard Klein, who has served as principal for the High School of Music and Art since 1968. In the expanded school Richard Klein plans a curriculum which will be integrated with the professional performances taking place at Lincoln Center. Classes will attend rehearsals of the N.Y. Philharmonic orchestra, the Metropolitan Opera and the American Ballet Theatre. Students may take part in some of the performances, and many of the celebrated artists who come to perform at Lincoln Center will conduct workshops for the students of the La Guardia High School.

How could I have dreamed back in 1934, during the first days of La Guardia's administration, that my simple, practical suggestion made out of a restless concern for gifted students would result in the creation of an institution to contribute new dimensions to the field of music and art education and set a precedent for schools throughout the nation?

What the High School of Music and Art has accomplished is really a demonstration of the practical application of my long held belief in the importance of bringing students in their formative years into close contact with the best in music and art. This recognizing and training of gifted students has over the years resulted in the development of a special group of citizens whose appreciation of and participation in the arts has become one of our nation's great natural resources.

Throwing Out the First Violin

During the 1930s and '40s, when La Guardia was Mayor of New York, for six weeks each summer the N.Y. Philharmonic Orchestra gave a series of concerts at the low admission prices of 25 cents to one dollar at Lewisohn Stadium. This was a huge outdoor arena which served as the athletic field of the City College of New York, located adjacent to the school in a remote section of the Upper West Side. It was a cool refuge for the city's music lovers to bask in great music under the stars. During the nine years I served on the Board of Higher Education, which had jurisdiction over the College and its Stadium, I was designated to handle all matters relating to music, which included the concerts at Lewisohn Stadium. Minnie Guggenheimer, who presided over the outdoor concerts, put a plan into effect which offered free tickets to City College students. When I learned that very few of these free tickets were ever used, I put a charge of ten cents on each ticket. This resulted in thousands of them being purchased, and young people thronged to the concerts. For many of them it was their introduction to good music. I had taken a leaf out of my experience as a merchandiser which proved again that people place little value on anything they get for nothing.

The Summer Symphony concerts at Lewisohn Stadium became an important feature of life in New York. It had become a tradition for Mayor La Guardia to open each season by attending the first concert and making a few introductory remarks. He enjoyed driving with me to the Stadium in my open car, which he dearly loved.

One opening night, while driving to the Stadium with the Mayor, I somehow lost my way among the maze of narrow, unfamiliar streets at 138th Street and Convent Avenue in the City College area and suddenly found myself driving down a one-way street in the wrong direction. Naturally I was promptly spotted by a traffic policeman who ordered me to stop. Without glancing at my passenger, the officer launched into a stern lecture which he generously embellished with unprintable language. When I attempted to direct his attention to the presence of the Mayor in my car, Fiorello hushed me, saying:

"*Schweig. . . ruhig*" (Be quiet).

At this the officer recognized my distinguished companion and began to sputter and apologize. Fiorello hopped out of the car, cut the officer short with the words, "Lock him up!" and with a wave of his hand strode off in the direction of the Stadium.

Abandoned, and with the help of several officers including a few on horseback, I managed to maneuver my way back out of the one-way street until I was directed to the parking area of the Stadium.

I was unaware that the Mayor and a group of other City officials had gathered together to observe my frantic efforts, until I heard the Mayor announce in his high-pitched voice, loud enough to be heard by the gathering crowd en route to the Stadium, "What that guy needs is Randall's Island to turn around in."

I finally managed to extricate myself from the crowd, and reached my seat just in time to hear the Mayor on the stage turn to Minnie Guggenheimer, and in the grand tradition of the opening game of the baseball season, ask her for an extra fiddle . . . "so I can throw out the first violin. . . ."

"We Save Them First and Argue After"

The United Nations Relief and Rehabilitation Administration is the least heralded, yet noblest contribution of one of America's most remarkable citizens. What La Guardia had accomplished within the limited geography of New York City as mayor, he now expanded to encompass the entire world community. His brilliant guidance and tireless execution of the vast and complex UNRRA operation resulted in the rescue and restoration of tens of thousands of lost, starving, homeless and despairing victims of World War II.

A few short months after La Guardia left City Hall in 1946, President Truman personally called upon him to take over and re-organize the demoralized UNRRA. The organization was failing in its vital task of caring for and feeding the millions of lost, starving and displaced persons in post-war Europe. Something had to be done quickly, and President Truman turned to La Guardia to take on the monumental rescue task, which was analogous but multiple in size to the one so brilliantly performed by Herbert Hoover after World War I.

Having completed five terms in Congress and twelve tumultuous years as Mayor of New York, La Guardia had looked forward to a period of well deserved rest away from public life. He had serious misgivings about accepting this overwhelmingly demanding post and invited me to come to his home to discuss it. I strongly urged him to accept President Truman's appeal in view of his deep sympathy and vast experience in organization especially for the underprivileged. I buttressed my argument with the slogan I had used during my wartime rescue operations in Turkey: "WE SAVE THEM FIRST AND ARGUE AFTER."

On March 29, 1946, La Guardia became Director General of UNRRA. Within twenty-four hours the hammer blows of his direction began to be felt. Ships laden with food en route to countries where the need was less urgent were re-routed at sea and diverted to areas where the need was greater. He turned to me to take on a mission to the Middle East and also to make a survey of the Displaced Persons camps in Germany. I can almost hear the staccato phrases he barked at me before I left. "Our first task, Ira, is to break up the red tape, to discard the rules. Improvise in any way you can on your mission. We must get the food to the starving people."

The story of my experiences as a Special Inspector General of UNRRA to rescue the surviving remnants of the war in Displaced Persons camps, has been told in a separate chronicle I wrote, entitled *The Embers Still Burn,** which did not include several episodes in which music played a colorful part.

In Europe, Meyer Cohen, another special assistant to La Guardia, and I arranged to have the UNRRA private plane at our disposal to expedite our movements from one European capital to another with my staff of about a half dozen men and women of various nationalities.

The emotional drain of close daily contact with the war's scarred and desolate humans had left me in a state of extreme exhaustion every night. In desperation I turned to my one sure source of balm—music. When in Frankfurt, I attended a performance of Verdi's *Un Ballo in Masquera* in a bombed out opera house that had been partially reconstructed. The high-level performance from a stage in battered condition seemed almost miraculous. Upon inquiry, I learned that the Opera Houses in other cities on our itinerary had also been among the first buildings to be rebuilt and performances were being revived. I took advantage of our military signal system to send a message each day to the city we were to visit next, requesting the title of the opera to be performed there that evening. As a result, when we landed in Berlin, Munich, etc., as the door of the plane opened I would be greeted by a military guard who would salute smartly with one word, *Tosca* or *Otello*, or *Tannhäuser*, whatever opera was scheduled for the night.

When we arrived in Munich, I invited the members of my staff to join me at the opera, as we were to have the use of the ornately decorated Royal box originally reserved for the King of Bavaria, later taken over by Adolf Hitler and his entourage. The box was spacious enough to include an area

* Simon & Schuster, 1949.

in the rear for food and drink. It did not occur to me that the members of my staff might have preferred to rest or to retreat to some less erudite form of evening relaxation. I confess to having had a special feeling of satisfaction in knowing that I was replacing Hitler and his General Staff in the luxurious loge while enjoying a stirring performance of Verdi's *Otello*.

During the death scene at the climax of the opera, I glanced over my shoulder, expecting to see the members of my staff caught up in the magic of the music. Instead, there they were, relaxed in their comfortable chairs in strangely awkward positions, fast asleep, their occasional snores an obligato to the eloquence of the rapturous Verdi pouring out from the stage. Noting the expressions of benign contentment on their faces, I took a measure of satisfaction from the thought that the music which had aroused me to a state of ecstasy had also served them well, but as a soothing lullaby.

The relaxation from the opera did not serve to interfere with the regular 6:00 A.M. awakening of the UNRRA team next morning to continue our relentless search for lost children and our efforts to heal their wounds.

Among my happiest memories of the period of the 1930s and early '40s are the hilarious Saturday evenings I spent with La Guardia and his friends at his home at Gracie Mansion and in Riverdale. He would enjoy presiding as a master cook, complete with white apron and chef's cap, surrounded in the kitchen by his friends, including Sidney Hillman, Morris Novick, Adolph Berle, Newbold Morris and Ernest Gruening.

The Mayor loved to embellish his culinary skills with impromptu performances, which included his twirling a razor-sharp steak knife into the air. We would hold our collective breath until he caught the instrument by its wooden handle, followed by a low bow. The preliminary raucousness of the parties, well lubricated by the scotch and soda which preceded the dinners, was amiably tolerated by La Guardia's inimitable wife, Marie.

In November of 1946, with La Guardia's assumption of the UNRRA post, the celebrated Saturday evenings came to an abrupt halt. Working with him at his feverish pace, I could not help observing with sad awareness the gradual depletion of his once irrepressible energy. When La Guardia returned from his last tour of Europe and Asia, I met him at the airport. In two months he had covered the entire area of my preparatory mission in Germany as well as the Soviet Union. I was shocked to see the change in him in so short a time, as the dread disease that would soon claim his life was rapidly overtaking him. It was a heartbreaking sight.

In his final weeks at home, I joined Marie and their two adopted children, Jean and Eric, in efforts to distract him from the pain of his terrible illness. Having experienced with him over the years the joy that music brought him, I turned to Jean to join me in playing unrehearsed piano duets by Franz Schubert on the Steinway in his living room. As our lone audience, the great man would sit wrapped in his bathrobe, huddled on a nearby couch. As we played, I stole a glimpse at him and could see that, lost in the music, his eyes had for the moment recaptured the look of radiance I had known so well.

That the anguish of the man of great heart and prodigious accomplishment could even for a brief moment be relieved by the blessings of music I helped bring to his home, is for me a consoling memory.

Chapter Eight

WABF-FM—Dream Station

Atop the forty-one story Hotel Pierre on Fifth Avenue and Sixty-first Street in New York, a giant antenna pierces the sky, a relic of my experimental television station W2XMT and FM radio station WABF-FM.

In 1939 I was advised by engineers to find the highest and most unimpeded spot on the New York skyline on which to build an antenna. One day, looking out of my office window at Bloomingdale's on Lexington Avenue and Fifty-ninth Street, I spotted the tower of the Hotel Pierre just two blocks away. (Later engineers congratulated me on having made one of the best technical guesses of the day.) The antenna stands there today, a mocking symbol of my early pioneering in the field of television, which in 1939 I was convinced was "just around the corner." I was of course far ahead of my time.

Back in 1929, at my urging, the engineers at radio station WOR in Newark, New Jersey succeeded in sending a flickering picture as far as Hackensack, New Jersey, a distance of about fifteen miles. At that time the accomplishment was considered so newsworthy that *The New York Times* published the story on its front page. It took ten more years of technical development, however, before the RCA company was able to demonstrate successfully the transmission of clear pictures via television to the public. At the 1939 New York World's Fair, RCA included in its exhibition a televised broadcast of a speech by President Franklin D. Roosevelt.

In that same year I secured an experimental license for the Metropolitan

Television Company, a subsidiary formed by Bloomingdale's and Abraham & Straus, both members of the Federated Department Store chain.

At the same time, I obtained television licenses for the other member stores of the Federated chain: Burdines in Miami, Filenes in Boston, Foley's in Houston, Lazarus in Columbus, Ohio, and Shilito's in Cincinnati.

The Federal Communications Commission demanded that specific requirements be met before giving the license final approval, which included presentation of a proposed program schedule and engineering specifications as proof of each store's intention of developing and operating a station. I submitted a budget of approximately three million dollars for all the stores to the Board of Federated Stores. But the bankers who dominated the Board expressed serious reservations about the expenditure of such a sum for a medium which, they contended, had yet to prove its "popular acceptance and profitability."

My plans and budget were rejected by the Board with the statement: "We think we'll stick to the retail business." This meant the abandonment of television licenses of prodigious potential value which I had obtained only after unrelenting efforts and through contacts at high levels in Washington. When I left the Board room, my final statement was: "Gentlemen, you have just dissipated assets which have a future value that will some day exceed that of your stores."

My clear vision of the future of television was blocked by the dismal myopia of the bankers and corporate bosses, who with one sweeping decision had squandered the assets worth many millions which I had brought within their reach. Some years later, the late eminent merchant Fred Lazarus, Jr., Chairman of Federated Stores, who had been the lone dissenter and the only one of his colleagues who supported me, generously acknowledged for the record that the Board had been short-sighted. In a letter to me he wrote: "Had we listened to you, Ira, back in 1939, our businesses would now be worth many times their present value."

To assist me in obtaining the television licenses, I had engaged a brilliant young attorney, Andrew G. Haley. One day, in his office in Washington, he casually brought up the name of Major Edwin H. Armstrong. Haley revealed that Armstrong in his laboratory had succeeded in developing a revolutionary new system of radio transmission. The name "Armstrong" rang a bell; I knew he was the inventive genius who had developed the first effective radio receiver and whose technological contributions had made possible radio broadcasting as we know it. When I learned that Armstrong's new system would eliminate static, distortion and the other interferences which then plagued radio sound, my enthusiasm went into high gear. The prospect of a system of radio transmission that could capture the pure sound of music from the ether diverted me from my concentration on television, and I was off to visit Armstrong in his basement laboratory at Columbia University.

Armstrong's demonstration of his startling new system left no doubt in my mind that it was nothing short of a revolution over the limited AM (Amplitude Modulation) method of broadcasting then in general use. As soon as I heard the clear, unmuffled sound of music from his new system and learned that Armstrong, too, was a passionate music lover, we became kindred spirits, and I allied myself with him in the development and promotion of his new system, which he called Frequency Modulation (FM).

Under the aegis of the Metropolitan Television Company, I quickly applied for and received one of the first licenses for FM radio granted in New York. I had an antenna for FM broadcasting erected atop the Hotel Pierre, which already housed W2XMT, the experimental television station. I called the FM radio station W75NY, "The Information Station," and alternated programs of great music with information on important events and background material on the news of the day. The station began broadcasting in November of 1942 and continued through the war years. I kept it functioning as a "holding operation" while I served as a United States emissary in Turkey. But in my absence the store's management lost interest in the station, and when I returned to the United States in 1945, with the generous financial assistance of Harry Scherman, the astute creator and chairman of the Book-of-the-Month Club, I bought both the television and the FM station from the department stores. For the first time in my life I became the head of my own business. I redesignated the radio station as WABF, dedicated it to programs of great music, and we resigned ourselves to financial losses during the first years of operation.

The enormous costs and competition with New York's major television stations, along with the concentration on the development of WABF, convinced me to abandon my experimental television license. The FM radio station was to be the medium through which I could expand the formula for bringing the best music to the public, which had been so successful with the New Friends of Music. No longer would I be limited to a weekly concert of one and a half hours, but would have access to eight hours a day for seven days a week. It was obvious that FM was the perfect medium for chamber music. To quote the eminent composer and music critic Virgil Thomson, "Chamber music was written to be heard in a kind or semi-privacy, and now could be heard as it should be heard, in everyone's home where it is at home."

I published a "Statement of Aims" (see illustration) explaining that the station's credo was to eliminate many of the abuses which had fastened onto the radio industry, citing the frequent interruptions for loud and often repetitive commercial announcements. Here was the opportunity to implement my belief that broadcasting, once freed from these sins, could soar to new heights as an instrument for the faithful transmission of music, education and enlightenment.

It was an uphill struggle from the start, a break from the established order in broadcasting. But we were encouraged by signs of appreciation of our innovations and high standards from such important sources as *The New York Times*, *The Saturday Review of Literature* and *The Reader's Digest*, which published an article entitled:

> Radio as It Should Be
> Something New on the Air
> A Station that Respects Its Listeners.

Quotes from *The Reader's Digest* article are as valid today as a credo for a "Dream Station" as when published in January 1950:

> People in and around New York have been listening to something almost too good to be true, a radio station with good manners.
>
> FM station WABF tiptoes in with well-chosen music and then steps back to let you enjoy it.
>
> WABF behaves like a guest in your home.
>
> WABF was started to broadcast good music and to present it courteously. On conventional stations long musical compositions are often cut so they will end on the hour or half hour, on WABF all numbers are played through without interruption, regardless of time.
>
> Commercials never take more than two minutes for every 60 minutes of music, much less time than on most stations, and they wait till the end of a long composition.
>
> WABF announcers are forbidden under pain of dismissal to punch the advertising message into the mike. They may recommend, they may suggest; they may not wheedle or bully the listeners. The radio station is merely the intermediary between Beethoven and the public. The broadcaster must talk as he would in a friend's living room.
>
> WABF is estimated to have close to 200,000 listeners, which makes it the best attended purely FM station in or around New York."
>
> It has a mouthpiece, the monthly *Program Magazine* which, in addition to listing all the compositions programmed, publishes editorials and articles on music.
>
> Its small staff of 30 is a compatible team of individuals united by a love and knowledge of music ... even the porter plays the violin.

We received several honors· The Department of State singled out WABF's concert programs for rebroadcasting to listeners throughout the world. In 1950, WABF received the George Foster Peabody Award (radio's Oscar) for "the integrity of its musical presentations ... for creating in WABF a unique, relaxing and reliable treasure house."

In *The New York Times* of December 28, 1947, an Honor Roll for accomplishments in the field of radio was published, in which WABF was cited as follows:

> Frequency Modulation: In the newest aural art of radio, Ira Hirschmann and his station WABF, displayed the most original and intelligent pro-

gramming logically. Its many fine musical offerings, highlighted by the concerts of the New Friends of Music, have been conceived with both imagination and taste and represent an important addition to what radio has to offer.

I engaged Ignace Strasfogel as Music Director who later became a conductor at the Metropolitan Opera. Together we set our sights on creating programs which respected the intelligence of our listeners. On Sunday evenings WABF broadcast the full concerts of the New Friends of Music, direct from Town Hall without interruption for commercial announcements.

As a member of New York's Board of Higher Education, which had jurisdiction over Hunter College, I was able to introduce the first Opera workshop into the school. WABF broadcast the workshop's programs on a regular schedule.

Another innovation was the monthly *WABF Program Magazine*, which listed the full schedule of programs for the coming month and included interesting and informative music articles written by such leading musicologists as Konrad Wolff, Paul Rosenfeld, Isidore Phillip, Virgil Thomson, Irving Kolodin and Olin Downes. Only recently, after many years, have program magazines become regular features of other radio stations, notably WQXR and WNCN. Public television's Channel Thirteen has also adopted this idea, which seemed logical and obvious as far back as at that time.

The *WABF Program Magazine* listed only the approximate time of the forthcoming programs, as I refused to constrict them to conform to precise split-second timing. To allow our music performers and speakers complete relaxation, they were permitted to run over their allotted time briefly when necessary, a violation of one of radio's most sacred precepts. Occasionally, when a program did run overtime and delayed the one next scheduled, the station would receive telephone complaints. One evening I listened in on a call from an irate lady in New Jersey who demanded to know why the music that was scheduled was not yet on the air. A performance of the Schubert Trio Opus 99 was running several minutes overtime. Taking over the phone I asked her politely, "Madam, what better use could you possibly make of two minutes than to hear the complete and unhurried ending of a Schubert

Trio?" The unmistakable click of the receiver was her only reply. Another time a call from Princeton, New Jersey was switched to my line. When the voice on the other end gave the name Albert Einstein in a German accent, I hesitated for a moment. But when the great mathematical genius asked whether the Beethoven piece just broadcast was in the key of C-sharp or C-sharp Minor, I recalled that Professor Einstein was a music lover who played the violin and was a member of a chamber music group.

In spite of the many expressions of appreciation from our listeners, and the plaudits and honors we received from critics and musicians, my aims and ideals for WABF ran headlong into the realities of commercialism.

At the time, the giant RCA company dominated the field of communications. The parent company of NBC, the major network, it was also one of the major manufacturers of receiving sets and controlled most of the essential AM patents, all of which produced immense profits.

When David Sarnoff, who had been a longtime friend of Major Armstrong and an original sponsor of his FM system, attempted to buy the FM patent rights from the inventor, who rebuffed his offer, a bitter and long drawn-out court battle followed which left the former friends implacable enemies.

It is hoped that some day the full story of Armstrong's agonizing struggle against the corporate powers will be told. But this is not the place to detail how the man who pioneered radio broadcasting was blocked in his efforts to bring his superior FM system to the people.

The key victim of the derailment of FM was Major Armstrong himself. His long legal battle with RCA left him embittered and exhausted, mentally as well as financially, and in 1951 he took his own life.

I was among the victims caught in the FM crossfire. To put WABF on a solid footing, it was necessary to have a sufficiently wide listening audience to attract advertisers. But although an increasing audience of sensitive listeners was beginning to request FM sound, the limited number of receiving sets being produced by the manufacturers was not only overpriced but mechanically flawed. By design or accident, the FM signal would "drift," forcing listeners to make constant hand adjustments on their radio dials. It would take years before usable sets were produced in quantity at a price within the reach of the average pocketbook.

Although WABF had the largest listening audience on any FM station, it operated at an annual loss of about $50,000.

Meanwhile I had learned that there was not a sufficient quantity of great classical music to fill a broadcast schedule consistently for eight hours a day, seven days a week. But I refused to compromise my standards by adding mediocre music fare, or to offer "mixed programming" and offensive, ill-timed selling messages.

The following is a quote from one of the many letters we received from listeners which encouraged me to maintain my standards.

> We have never written to a radio station before but feel that WABF should receive some acknowledgment of its fine work.... Your programs, especially chamber music, are superb and imaginative. We like the relaxed atmosphere of WABF, one program flows smoothly into the next and the commercials are restrained.
>
> We are not musicians but ordinary people who love good music and WABF is a real music lover's station. This letter is an attempt to tell you of our appreciation for the high caliber of your programs and to express our thanks.

Rather than abandon my "Dream Station," I decided to offer WABF to the United Nations as an outright gift.

I met with Dag Hammarskjold, Secretary-General of the UN, a statesman in his own right, and together we set up the machinery for transferring all of the WABF equipment from the top of the Hotel Pierre to the roof of the UN building on the East River. I supplied the UN with a complete format for disseminating programs of information, good music, background materials on the member nations and a system for the multi-lingual coverage of the meetings of the General Assembly, the Security Council and other major committees. I insisted that the transfer take place with no fanfare or personal reference to me. At the last minute, however, and with no explanation, I was told that the gift would have to be rejected. I did learn unofficially that the Soviet

Union had objected on the grounds that a station in New York would not be able to maintain political objectivity.

Eventually the station was sold to a group who turned it into a public-supported station with the new call letters WBAI. Almost ten years would pass before the sheer weight of demand by audiences for better music would cause the manufacturers to capitulate and offer the public FM sets that worked. Today the American people at last are getting undistorted and static-free music as the standard of broadcasting so long denied them. But hard is the road of the pioneer.

On a lighter note I cannot restrain the temptation to recall an accidental episode which served in a minor way to assuage my anguish for having initiated an enterprise that was so far ahead of its time. It is connected with my last visits to the tower that housed what I called the station's laboratory in the sky. The last floor in the Hotel Pierre reached by elevator was used as a banquet hall. From there, to reach the station one had to climb a flight of stairs to the studio in the tower. One late afternoon, as I emerged from the elevator, the hand of a uniformed waiter reached out to me, and before I could question him, he offered me a drink from a tray. The sound of a dance band revealed that a reception was in full swing in the banquet hall, and I had obviously been mistaken for one of the guests.

Instinctively, I accepted the drink (a cool martini), and went into the ballroom to mingle with the crowd, an uninvited guest. Later, on other trips to the tower, when receptions were taking place I could not resist the temptation to take advantage of this impromptu hospitality, reflecting that the half million dollar loss I had suffered with the station was being partially diluted by the only "liquidity" that WABF ever enjoyed.

Chapter Nine

Music in Ankara

Ankara Branch of The New Friends Music

The small lobby of the Ankara Palas Hotel in Ankara was a welcome haven after my ten-day flight on U.S. Army cargo planes through four continents. It was February 1944, and the war was roaring to a climax.

While checking in at the hotel desk, through the strange babble of the Turkish language around me, I was surprised to hear the unmistakable sounds of a Beethoven piano sonata coming from a nearby lobby. En route to my room, curiosity prompted me to peer into the small ballroom, where I recognized the figure of the eminent German artist Walter Gieseking at the piano. His audience comprised the members of the diplomatic corps. Seated in the front row was the notorious German Ambassador, Franz von Papen (the Fox). I had no difficulty in recognizing him, as in 1933 fate had conspired to have him seated next to me at a Music Festival in Salzburg, Austria. Our conversation was, as I recall, polite and confined to the music, but I had never forgotten his cold, unfeeling eyes.

What an unbelievable coincidence for me to have arrived in the capital of "neutral" Turkey at the very hour of a performance by the darling of the Nazis, Walter Gieseking. My memory flashed back to 1937 and an earlier encounter with the German pianist. I had engaged him to play for the New Friends of Music in New York, but upon learning of his alliance with

Hitler, I had canceled the engagement.

Gieseking performed exclusively on the piano produced by the Baldwin Co., which was then sponsoring the radio broadcasts of the New Friends of Music concerts. Upon learning of my cancellation of Gieseking's appearance, the Baldwin Company withdrew their sponsorship of the broadcasts, causing me a substantial financial loss. Now here in far-off Ankara, the shadow of Nazism was again pursuing me in the figure this time of Walter Gieseking, sponsored by one of the Third Reich's most cunning politicians. I was to tilt lances with the sixty-three-year-old ace German Ambassador throughout the time I spent in Ankara.

Von Papen had earned a reputation for almost unequaled perfidy back in the First World War when, as Kaiser Wilhelm's Ambassador, he had been expelled from the United States for recruiting young hoodlums to blow up the bridges and railways the U.S. used to transport weapons and material being sent to England and France. Now he was continuing his skullduggery in Ankara, where he had a staff of four hundred in addition to numerous collaborators. I later learned that it was due to his conniving that the S.S. Struma had been torpedoed carrying 775 Rumanian Jewish refugees to their doom. My rescue operations while in Turkey involved me in a continuous uphill struggle, mainly against the German Ambassador. While claiming "neutrality" during most of the war, Turkey was actually locked in a conspiratorial alliance with the Germans guided by the evil hand of Franz von Papen. When, in 1944, the tide of battle began to turn in favor of the Allies, the Turks almost overnight adroitly switched sides. I enjoyed observing the spectacle of the Germans' fall from grace as they lost their political grip on Turkey.

Another battle I had to fight in Ankara was against boredom. I found the capital of Turkey to be nothing more than a remote, overgrown village. Ankara had been selected by President Ataturk as the capital of his newly formed Republic because it was in the center of the country in a mountainous area of five thousand feet above sea level, which made it inaccessible to enemy attack in the era before airplanes came into common use.

Before I left New York, Bruno Walter had given me a letter of introduction to his friend Carl Ebert, Director of the Turkish School of Opera in Ankara, where he produced miracles with the primitive, untrained, youthful singers of the country; his production of Beethoven's difficult, heroic score of *Fidelio* with the raw, inexperienced Turkish vocalists was a masterpiece of inspired direction. Ebert had won world repute as director of the Glynbourne Opera in England and in a similar post in pre-Nazi Berlin. Though not a Jew, he had found refuge in Turkey after rejecting Hermann Goering's urgent and flattering offers to remain in Germany as Director of German Theater and Opera. In Ankara, he and his charming wife, Gertie, provided a civilized refuge for me in their home. They introduced me to Gilbert Back, a distinguished violinist who because of his Jewish background had been dismissed from the Berlin Philharmonic Orchestra by Wilhelm Furtwängler.

To break the monotonous routine of diplomatic social life in Ankara, I suggested to Back that he form a string quartet which I would sponsor. He promptly hired three Turkish instrumentalists and began rehearsing Beethoven and Mozart quartets in preparation of a program to be performed at a reception I was planning to give for the members of the diplomatic corps. I decided to offer a chamber music concert as the appropriate level on which to bring the diplomats of the world together.

Gilbert Back ran into less harmony than he had anticipated with the three Turkish string players. Unaccustomed to discipline, occasionally in the middle of a rehearsal one of them would simply put down his instrument and casually meander off, leaving his companions stranded, thus ending the session.

Back was a tireless taskmaster, and I too rode herd on the Turkish musicians, lavishing them with "baksheesh" in return for additional hours of rehearsal.

At one point Back ran out of patience and threatened to disband the quartet. I was in Istanbul when he phoned me, interrupting a crucial meeting with members of the Turkish government, where I was negotiating for the purchase of ships from the Turkish navy for my rescue operations. I managed to pacify Back and cajole him into continuing his efforts to reconcile the discords of Asia Minor with the harmony of Mozart in C-sharp Major.

Finally Back informed me that the quartet was ready for a concert. This was the moment I had waited for, to repay with my own kind of reception all of the hospitality that had been so relentlessly forced upon me. In exchange for the round of stodgy dinners and cocktail parties I had endured at the various Embassies, I would give a chamber music concert in the very same hall of the Ankara Palas Hotel where I had found Walter Gieseking performing for the diplomatic corps at the reception given by the German Ambassador on the day of my arrival in Ankara. Now a string quartet representing my New Friends of Music would upstage Franz von Papen and his Nazi cohort, Gieseking.

I was determined to make my reception a memorable event in all respects. I entrusted the gourmet Joe Levy, correspondent of *The New York Times* in Ankara, with all the arrangements for food and drink. He did so nobly. Dulcie Steinhardt, wife of the regular Ambassador to Turkey, saw to it that all of the diplomats and Turkish government officials were seated according to protocol. I personally arranged for the printing of the invitations, not a simple task as available facilities for printing in English were somewhat rudimentary. After a number of revisions the invitations were printed and mailed out (complete with a misspelling of Beethoven). I included the musical program of the evening on the invitation under the proud heading of the name: "New Friends of Music of New York, U.S.A., Ankara Branch."

As in my New York concerts I announced that the program would begin on time and that there would be no interruptions between movements. The British Ambassador, Sir Hugh Knatchball-Huggesson, Von Papen's opposite number, arrived late and was obliged to remain outside the hall until the Beethoven was finished. Only years later, when his secret dispatches were released, did I learn that he had complained bitterly about "the arrogant young American diplomat and his disturbing operations."

The evening proved to be both a diplomatic triumph and an artistic tour de force. After the concert, in the mellow mood generated by the music, an informal meeting of the minds of the diplomats took place, in which some knotty misunderstandings which had existed between the Turkish hierarchy and our government were successfully reconciled. Standing around the piano, drinks in hand as ensigns of conviviality, we exchanged views and agreed on terms. Once again it was music that had served magically to transform prior discords into mutual harmony.

When I returned to Ankara two years later in 1946 on a post-war mission for UNRRA, I learned that the string quartet which I had sponsored had continued as a unit and had flourished under Back's leadership. It was a joyful hour when on June 5, 1946, I heard my quartet, consisting of the same musicians, now ripened from years of performing together in a program of Mozart and Schubert, in the very same ballroom of the Ankara Palas Hotel. Could there be a more vivid example of the contagion and persistence of great music?

Impromptu Music in Casablanca

During the war, on one of my flights back to the States from Turkey, I found myself unexpectedly in the reverse role of being personally rescued as the result of an impromptu musical interlude.

When our plane made an overnight stop in Casablanca, I hoped to elude the routine army examination of my papers which included some personal and secret documents. But the prying eyes of the U.S. Army control at the airport permitted no exceptions for mere rank, especially in the case of a citizen not in uniform. My diplomatic passport and even my letter from President Roosevelt, which I brandished before the eyes of the Army inspector, were brushed aside with the rejoinder, "That means nothing to us. *We're* running the war here." Just as I was about to surrender my private papers, the soldier took a second look at my name and stopped short. He peered at me quizzically and said, "So you're Ira Hirschmann. You're a man I've been wanting to get in touch with for years, just to ask you one question. Why, at the opening concert of the New Friends of Music, did you put the most difficult of all Beethoven's music, the C Sharp Minor Quartet, as the very first number on the program?" When I explained that my reason for placing the most lofty music at the beginning of each concert program was that I wanted it to be heard when the audience was fresh and most receptive, he actually embraced me, saying, "You can bring any damn thing you want in with you." He then invited me to spend the night with him in his tent, where he had a phonograph and a treasure of chamber music records. We sat up through most of the night, listening and exulting in some of our favorite Beethoven and Mozart classics. Under the spell of the music and the raw red wine with which he plied me, our mood grew increasingly mellow as the hours folded into dawn.

Next morning, my newly acquired "friend of music" escorted me to my plane and I flew off, secret papers intact, literally on the wings of song.

Rescue in the American Embassy

In the restaurant of the Park Hotel where I stayed when I was in Istanbul, a trio of musicians consisting of two violinists and a cellist provided welcome dinner music each night. The first violinist, Mischa Friedman, a Jewish refugee from Vienna, and I came to know each other through my frequent requests for the trio to switch from its usual light repertoire to pieces by Schubert and Mozart. I was struck by the sound of Friedman's violin. It was unmistakably clear that he was performing on a beautiful instrument. When I complimented him on it, he proudly and lovingly displayed his violin to me.

When the tide of war turned decisively against the Germans, the Turks dropped their pretense of "neutrality" and announced that all nationals with German or Austrian passports, including refugees, were to be rounded up and interned in a camp located in a remote wooded area on the outskirts of Ankara.

Friedman, whose Austrian passport was stamped with a "J," was among those to be rounded up. One night, when I was working alone in the Embassy, I heard a rush of noise outside the front door. My violinist friend raced frantically into the building, clutching his violin case with a cadre of Turkish police at his heels.

"Quick, they're after me," he cried, and I slammed the Embassy door against the police. He was breathing hard and sweating as he gasped, "If I'm caught they'll take my violin and I'll give up my life before I give it up. Please take care of it for me." There was desperation in his eyes.

In spite of the cardinal rule that only those in the employ of the U.S. government could be permitted to occupy the Embassy premises, I pulled Friedman into the building, pushed him to the rear of the hall, and shoved him into a small room used for storage. I whispered to him to be quiet and to remain there until I knocked on the door. As the only official on the Embassy staff there at that late hour, and in a position of authority, I signaled to our watchman not to interfere. From my office window I watched until I saw the Turkish policemen finally give up and abandon their quest. Friedman remained inside the Embassy through the night until in the early hours of the morning I slipped my young friend safely out of the building, his arms lovingly embracing his violin case. No one ever learned that the sacrosanct premises of the American Embassy had served, involuntarily, as a sanctuary for one more Nazi-intended victim.

A few months later the Turks entered the war on the side of the Allies, and the refugees were released from the internment camp. One evening Friedman burst into the hotel dining room, his face radiant with smiles. We embraced and he insisted on playing a solo program of my Schubert and Mozart favorites.

Perhaps it was the mood of celebration, but the sound of Friedman's violin that evening still remains unforgettable to me. The joy of his playing reflected his gratitude for the liberation which his violin, a musical "passport," had won for him.

Beethoven's Stirring Chords

Before leaving the United States for Ankara in 1944, I met with the Secretary of Treasury, Henry Morganthau, Jr., in his office in Washington. There he pulled a large map from behind a curtain and pointed to an area of Rumania bordering the Soviet Union. He told me it was called Transnistria, and that 175,000 Rumanian Jews had been imprisoned there and were dying at the rate of 1,000 a day. In an off-hand manner the Secretary said, "While you are in Turkey, see what you can do to break up this concentration camp."

I also met with Carlos Davila, former Ambassador from Rumania to Washington, who had defected to the United States because of his opposition to his government's cooperation with the Nazis. He gave me a letter of introduction to his friend Alexandre Cretzianu, Rumanian Ambassador to Turkey.

In my desperate race against time while in Ankara, I decided to use Davila's letter for a top secret meeting with Cretzianu. At that very moment, American planes were bombing Rumania's Ploesti oil fields. Gilbert Simond, the Swiss Representative of the International Red Cross in Turkey, made all the arrangements for the secret meeting, which was to take place on a Saturday afternoon in Simond's home on the outskirts of Ankara.

Such a meeting involved enormous political risk, for I was constantly shadowed by German, Turkish, Japanese and British agents. I had been warned in Washington that if a meeting with an enemy came to light it would be flatly denied, my usefulness would be destroyed and I would be recalled by the State Department.

By agreement I arrived at Simond's home an hour before Cretzianu was due. I paced the floor of the modest living room, which was almost hermetically sealed by blinds until suddenly a grand piano in the corner of the room caught my eye. I succumbed to the temptation to reach for the keys, and my fingers almost automatically struck the introductory chords of the Beethoven sonata, Opus 90, so similar in their stirring proclamation to the opening chords of the *Fidelio* Overture.

Cretzianu turned out to be an urbane diplomat who spoke perfect English. When after about an hour of polite talk he mentioned the Russians, I reminded him that the Soviet armies were racing toward the Rumanian border and that he and his family were within weeks of being killed. The sudden breakdown of his polite armor prompted me to make a spontaneous, though unauthorized, offer of four secret American visas for himself, his wife and his two children in exchange for opening the door of the death camp in Transnistria, with the stipulation that first 5,000 children must immediately be released from the camp. I had little hope that my brash proposal would be approved by either the Rumanian or American governments, but a few days later the news reached me that 5,000 children had been released from Transnistria. The exchange had been accepted on my terms.

Unwilling to trust top secret information on a "deal" with an enemy ambassador to the regular cables, I flew back to the United States where, to my profound relief and gratitude, I was able to obtain President Roosevelt's secret approval of the issuance of the four American visas. The door of the death camp swung open, and the remaining victims, approximately 40,000, found their way to freedom.

Looking back on this episode, the most incredible of all my "crazy-quilt" experiences in the Middle East, I have never ceased asking myself what it was that gave me the audacity to concoct, offhand, such an unlikely offer to an enemy ambassador. Why was it that I did not hesitate or stop to calculate the perils involved in negotiations of such magnitude, or consider how remote the possibility was of such an exchange being accepted by the two warring governments? With the degree of tension that had been built up within me prior to the meeting, the confidence and conviction with which I faced him must have been derived from some outside source. I can only ascribe it, at least in part, to my brief session with the Beethoven score. I had approached the piano hesitantly, but the response, when my fingers touched the keys, was almost electric. My lungs, stifled by the tension that seemed to fill the narrow, darkened room, began to expand from the vibrations of the music. An overpowering sense of freedom from inhibition came over me. Suddenly it became overwhelmingly clear that here, facing me, was the one man who had the power to turn a key that would mean life instead of death to 40,000. Before I knew it, the bold offer exploded out of me.

What history will remember is not my spontaneous offer, or the escape of the four Rumanians, but the survival of the 40,000 remaining victims, and in retrospect I now know that the striking of those stirring Beethoven chords had emboldened me to throw caution to the wind and had been decisive for the lives of thousands.

Coda

I t is more than half a century since my courtship with music first began,
far back in time but propelled forward when measured in vision and faith.
Since then, that musical faith has touched the lives of people in many areas
of the world. The recent wide embrace of chamber music is one of the happiest symptoms of progress which has happened in spite of the bombast and
peril of our times.

No one could be so unrealistic as to believe that music alone could heal
the wounds of a society bleeding from its own excesses and miscalculations.
In an age of mounting tension and doubt there is an increased craving for
order and harmony. After a day of screaming headlines and vivid pictures
of murder and rape on the television sets right in our living rooms, a person
needs Bach and Beethoven.

The massive and growing pressures for material satisfactions have
led to more and more distortions and absence from order in our way of life.
Music is a mirror of the universal laws of nature. If the format of a great
music score provides no other basic lesson, it teaches us that without an
unalterable, essential form, it falls apart. View any Mozart score. It is in itself
a masterpiece of architectural design in notation and balance from which the
music seems ready to spring into orderly utterance. Yet it is the unending
variety within that order which makes for unity, not to be confused with uni-
formalization, a trap which reduces quality to quantity.

Leonardo da Vinci reminded us that our souls are composed of harmony, just as our bodies are a harmonious whole. Socrates, when stricken in his later years, learned to play the harp. The age-old healing and uplifting of music is as new as tomorrow.

Within all of us there is an unrequited yearning for serenity and harmony, expressed in our ever-present reach for light. When I listen to Mozart, my instinct is to turn, like a plant, toward its light, and a state of grace enlarges and sustains me; pettiness falls away into the lap of compassion. It is no accident that we speak of music touching the heart strings.

To have experienced the avidity with which a growing section of our people responded to music in its purest form, chamber music, has fortified my premise that people will listen to all music but will prefer the best. In 1936, my contention that there existed a sizable audience eager for chamber music was met with derision from friends who accused me of aiming "way above their heads." They were more farsighted than they intended, for the approximately 1,500 people who for eighteen years filled Town Hall for the concerts of the New Friends of Music heard music that did indeed lift them "above their heads," often reaching all the way to the heavens.

The New Friends of Music concerts opened up an entire new world of music's sublime literature to Americans, and became the springboard for this neglected art which is now an accepted part of the entire nation's repertoire. To counteract the endless outpourings of banal, raucous sound from radio, mass recordings and the frenzy of television still remains, as in all good things, an uphill struggle. But what that is worthwhile is not? Have any of the great reforms or civilizing tenets of our society come quickly or easily? Do we defy or sing of men of material wealth? Of what does the poet sing? Nations' songs are born out of the tradition of struggle, beauty and glory. Is Bismarck remembered above Beethoven? Schubert's "March Militaire" will be heard when Sherman's "March to the Sea" is dead history.

Mine is a voice keyed to music as a life-theme, always singing within me as a separate obligato of serenity. When I hear music I fear no danger; I am invulnerable. I am related to the earliest of times and the latest. Sometimes within a few bars of music lies an experience that can fill the gaps and omissions from an entire lifetime's earthly anguish and create an overwhelming sense of uplift and surcease. Besides the exaltation, I have found music to be a recipe for humility, the speediest cure for vanity. This disembodiment achieved from listening and hearing is a living reproach to today's purveyors of noise and discord and to the growing peril of the unifiers in science and computers. For a great problem of our time is the pressure to uniform us, and uniform is no form.

Picasso reminds us that only out of variety can life find unity and the release of creative power. Music has opened up for me a variety of unique opportunities in the remotest fields, from the concept for Fiorello La Guardia to create a High School of Music and Art all the way, 8,000 miles away, to Ankara, where a chamber music concert played a signal role in a diplomatic mission.

The living history of our times will be enshrined not in the passing political scene or in the vast halls of the Pentagon, but in the intimate concert halls where the timeless sounds of Beethoven and Schubert will continue to enrich the lives and spirits of new generations.

For one whose life has been ennobled through music, it has been a special joy to have sensed the yearnings of so many and to have shared in their fulfillment.